Don't Call Me
MOM

Don't Call Me MOM

How to Improve Your In-Law Relationships

Leah Shifrin Averick, A.M., L.C.S.W.

LIFETIME BOOKS, INC.
HOLLYWOOD, FLORIDA

Library of Congress Cataloging-in-Publication Data

Averick, Leah Shifrin.
    Don't call me mom : how to improve your in-law relationships / by Leah Shifrin Averick.
      p. cm.
    ISBN 0-8119-0836-4 (alk. paper)
    1. Parents-in-law -- United States. 2. Interpersonal relations -- United States.
  I. Title
  HQ759.8.A95   1996
  306.87--dc20   96-3864
                                                               CIP

Printed in Canada

• Endorsements •

"This book was so much fun to read that it took a while to realize how informative and helpful it really is. Anyone who has ever had a relative will discover himself or herself in these pages."
-- Arnold Goldberg, M.D., Professor of Psychiatry at Rush Medical College, and the author of *The Problem of Perversion: The View From Self-Psychology*

"Long overdue...a welcome first step in addressing a too long neglected subject."
-- Stephen Z. Cohen, Ph.D., University of Illinois, Jane Addams School of Social Work, co-author of *The Other Generation Gap*

"This book is essential for everyone practicing therapy or counseling."
--Abraham J. Twerski, M.D., Associate Professor of Psychiatry, University of Pittsburgh School of Medicine, author of *Lights Along the Way*

"Poignant and instructive...reading like a novel, this book helps us get in touch with our feelings and provides guidelines for clearer and productive exchanges..."
--Paul Gitlin, DSW, University of Chicago, School of Social Service Administration

"This is a warm, wise, informed discussion of relations within the contemporary family of adulthood. Averick's report will be helpful for family members, for professionals, and for scholars. A wealth of information gathered from family members provides the most comprehensive summary to date of the manner in which adults and their relatives get along."
-- Bertram Cohler, Ph.D., Professor of Psychiatry, Rush -Presbyterian-St. Luke's Medical Center, author of *Mothers, Grandmothers, and Daughters*

• Table of Contents •

"There is nothing new beneath the sun."
Ecclesiastes, 1:9

"When a man has a worried heart, speak to a friend."
Proverbs 12:25
interpreted in the
Gemorrah Yomah, 75 A

• Preface •

Since the first edition of my book was published, (*How In-Laws Relate: It's All Relative*), times have changed but family problems have not. What has changed is an openness to discuss all types of family problems on daily TV talk shows and sitcoms. As an invited in-law expert, I found that some shows had hardly enough time to explore the full scope of in-law problems, except to reveal the hurt and anger of the participants. The merit of these shows is that they make the public more aware of in-law problems. The viewers learn that they are not alone — the issues are universal and timeless and can be addressed. Remember, there is no right or wrong way to be an in-law. Furthermore, as psychoanalyst Arnold Goldberg, M.D. states, "There is no one size that fits all solutions to difficulties!"

When a couple marries, each partner needs to feel that he[1] is the most important person to his spouse. This feeling grows between husband and wife whenever each considers the other's needs and wishes before those of anyone else. The tugs and pulls from the in-laws may not seem so intrusive when each spouse knows that he is valued and appreciated, "number one" as far as the other is concerned.

But the tensions exist. They exist even with parental approval as in arranged marriages. When the inevitable strains in in-law relations do occur, they may be eased by discussing them with one's spouse, as discussed in more detail in Chapter X, THE IN-LAW TRIANGLE. Because many couples are very sensitive about discussing their parents or siblings with each other, it may be easier to talk to a trusted confidant (friend, relative, or even therapist when necessary). Being listened to and understood is as essential to survival and solving problems as having oxygen to breathe. Talking enables you to clarify issues and get a different perspective. But be wary of confidants who incite and goad you to anger because of their own unmet needs.

Talking about problems with others may not be enough to solve them. What may also be helpful is to understand what motivates human behavior. Most people are driven by the need to be important and appreciated. This need is often fulfilled when one is listened to and treated with respect. Knowing this may be helpful to understand where the in-laws are coming from and what causes their behavior. Hopefully, using an empathic approach will diminish in-law tensions.

---

[1] To eliminate awkwardness, I will use the term "he" to refer to both male and female.

• Foreword •

TO: Leah Shifrin Averick
FROM: Jeffrey Zaslow
        Advice Columnist, *Chicago Sun-Times*

A daughter-in-law complains: "My husband and I have been married for 11 years, but my mother-in-law still displays photos of his ex-girlfriends all over her house. Isn't it time for her to put away that prom picture with good old Mindy?"

A son-in-law is annoyed that his father-in-law always wants to toss around a football. "I'm not athletic and I'm not interested. Why do I have to be the son he never had?"

A mother-in-law feels hurt that her daughter-in-law keeps her at arm's length. "How can I become friends with a daughter-in-law who is incredibly devoted to her mother?"

As an advice columnist, I've received hundreds of questions like these. In-law issues are among the most common (and the most hurtful) issues I'm asked to address. Sometimes, I can give advice based on experience. I am a veteran son-in-law. I am a loyal son of a mother-in-law. I am the devoted husband of a respectful daughter-in-law. I am the devoted husband of a respectful daughter-in-law. And as the father of three small girls, I suspect that someday I'll be a suspicious father-in-law.

But though I've learned from the in-law relationships in my life, and think they're healthy, I relate. That's why, many times in my work as an advice columnist, I've turned for guidance to the book you're now holding. Leah Shifrin Averick — whose warmth, concern and savvy come through as soon as you meet her — looks at the in-law bonds and binds with a sense of empathy and a sense of humor. She's smart and direct without pretending to be a know-it-all. She has revised her book to include a helpful chapter on keeping in-law children in mind (or at bay) when writring a will.

Many of the readers who write to me would be helped by reading this book, and I've told them so. Consider these questions I've received:

— "How can I deal with my mother-in-law's racism? When a relative sold her home to a black couple, my mother-in-law asked 'How dark are they?' How can I keep such hateful attitudes from my impressionable young son?" (Check out Averick's Chapter XVI: *Strategies for Coping.*)

— "Once, when visiting my mother-in-law's home, I went to the bathroom and left her in charge of my two-year-old son. I got out to find my son standing alone at the top of the stairs. (He can't walk down stairs without help.) When I rushed to him, my mother-in-law admonished me for being too cautious. 'Those stairs are carpeted,' she said. 'How could he hurt himself? And if he fell, he'd learn to be careful. Stop babying him!' How can I cope with such a woman?" (Read Averick's Chapter XIV: *In-Laws as Grandparents.*)

— "My daughter-in-law calls me by my first name. I love her like a daughter. Can't she find it in her heart to call me mom?" (Averick devotes a whole chapter to just this question — Chapter VI.)

Sure, sometimes I can toss out a pithy answer in my column.

"Dear Zazz: Every time my mother-in-law visits, she snoops around the house asking questions: 'How much does thos cost? How much does that cost?' It's like she's appraising everything we have. How can I respond?"

I advised: "Next time your mother-in-law asks, 'How much does this cost?' politely respond: 'I'm sorry, it's not for sale,' "

That answer works fine as entertainment in an advice column. But, of course, in the complicated world of in-law relationships, a bit more advice is in order. In fact, a truly proper response to the question above — to all the questions above — could fill a book. Averick has written just such a book. And we all can benefit from the lessons and wisdom she shares on the pages that follow.

• A Letter to the Author •

Once again, I have had the pleasure of reading your book, *Don't Call Me Mom: How To Improve Your In-Law Relationships*. I enjoyed it immensely and found it a most readable book. It is filled with practical insights and clinical pearls that both the professional and the lay person will find useful. I felt myself personally relating to a number of issues you raised, as well as drawing parallels from cases within my own clinical practice. Struggles over intergenerational separation and the appropriate rules of intergenerational distance are quite common in my couple and family therapy work.

I think this "how to" guide will be helpful to both couples and in-laws of any age, or for that matter anyone trying to cope with these age-old intergenerational issues. In particular, this book should be mandatory reading for prospective couples and in-laws. The insights you offer can help prevent in-laws from becoming outlaws!

Shalom Feinberg, M.D.
Assistant Clinical Professor of Psychiatry,
Albert Einstein College of Medicine

• Acknowledgments •

I dedicate the second edition of my book
to the memory of my father,
Rabbi Yehudah Leib Hikel Shifrin, Z'L,
who called this book,
"A SHALOM BAIS book,
a book to bring peace into the home."

I am indebted to my husband, children, children-in-law, ex-daughter-in-law, siblings, kin, friends, and strangers who were candid and generous as they shared their in-law experiences with me.

Thank you Neil Mermelstein for careful and logical editing; Elisha Prero and Alan Maclin for enthusiastic help when I was discouraged; Marcy Sugar for co-writing the questionnaire; friends who sustained me while data gathering for this edition — Rifka and Rabbi Yehoshua H. Eichenstein, Chana Greenberg, Malka Gluck, Lucille Jones, Blanche Keno, Millie Klitenick, Helen Kossoff and all the members of the Grassfield Writers' Collective.

• Editor's Statement •

We can choose our friends but not our family. The same may hold true with in-laws. True, we get to select who we are going to marry, but we cannot choose the in-laws that come along with a prospective spouse. So, where does one turn to for guidance when it comes to handling all the sticky, touchy and often confrontational situations that arise between in-laws?

There is hope. *Don't Call Me Mom* offers expert advice on how to improve your in-law relationships. If you have a problem with your in-laws or you want to avoid one and improve the lines of communication, this book will serve you well.

Who needs to make sure their in-laws don't become outlaws? Any couple getting married will want to consult this book. Newlyweds will find this advice invaluable. Indeed, anyone looking to improve their relationship with family members where stress or strain exists, will find this book invaluable.

Don't Call Me Mom is the only primer on in-law relationships. No other book is on the market that addresses the subject of in-laws and the needs of family relationships. Her teachings extend to anyone who is engaged, married, divorced or re-married — and their families.

How do you get the people you love to love each other — or at least not hate one another? It is not easy and sometimes it is plain impossible. But in many situations, by applying the advice of Mrs. Averick, you will see improvements in your family relationships. The success of your marriage may depend on your achieving peace and harmony with the in-laws.

There's nothing like family, for better or for worse. Whether you are born — or marry — into them, there is no turning back. Even in cases of death, divorce or illness, the ties that bind will always exist. The importance and value to have a loving, caring and sharing family can never be underestimated.

I enjoyed editing Mrs. Averick's book and learned new methods to approach old problems. I have no doubt you will find many tips and strategies to apply to your particular situation. You are in good hands with Leah Shifrin Averick, A.M., L.C.S.W.

Mrs. Averick is a clinical social worker in the private practice of psychotherapy. She has appeared as an in-laws relationship expert on all major national television and radio talk shows, including OPRAH, DONAHUE, GERALDO, JOAN RIVERS SHOW, JOAN LUNDEN and MONTEL WILLIAMS. She has been featured in *USA Today, The New York Times, Bride's Magazine, Bottom Line, The Washington Post, L.A. Times, The Chicago Tribune, McCall's* and all leading news publications.

Lifetime Books wishes you luck in your pursuit of family happiness. Please let us know how your relationships improved with the aid of this book by writing to Leah Averick, c/o Lifetime Books, 2131 Hollywood Blvd., Hollywood, FL 33020.

-- Brian Feinblum
Senior Editor
Lifetime Books

• Introduction •
Why I Wrote This Book

> *Peace will come to the world when*
> *daughters-in-law get along with mothers-in-law.*
> **MENEKET RIFKA, 16th-century**
> **Yiddish writer and educator**

> *A man is obligated to honor his father-in-law*
> *as much as his father.*
> **MEDRASH**

The phone rang. It was an overseas collect call from my son telling me, "Mom, I'm engaged." Instead of saying, "Mazel Tov, congratulations," I began asking him questions: "Who is she? Where did you meet her? What do you like about her? What kind of family does she come from?"

For days afterward, rather than feel elated by the news, I felt dazed. Was I in shock because of the suddenness of the news? Was I hurt because he had not consulted me before making his decision? Or was I simply not yet ready to become a mother-in-law?

I wondered if my parents were surprised when I told them I was engaged. I also wondered if all parents feel this way when their children announce their engagement.

As a teacher and psychotherapist specializing in adult and geriatric problems, I have taught and counseled people about a wide variety of personal and family problems. Yet I found myself at a loss as to what to do.

Though I had been both daughter-in-law and sister-in-law, I was like those people before Newton who saw apples fall from trees yet never thought about why they fell. I had never before thought about the dynamics of in-law relationships.

The more I thought about it, the more I began to see that when a couple marry, they form a relationship that includes not just the two of them but also their in-laws — the mother, father, brothers, and sisters of each spouse. Alive or dead, living near or far, they all influence the marriage, for better or for worse. As shown by the following sketch, this relationship can be quite complex:

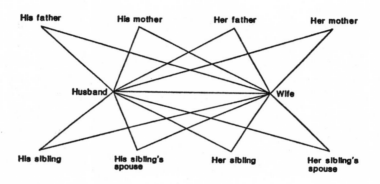

Now that I was to become a mother-in-law, I realized that my relationship with my son would be changing and that new people would be entering my life. I had to understand more.

Since I had no protocol to guide me, I decided to read how others had handled themselves in similar circumstances. I searched the libraries but found very few books or magazine articles on in-law relationships. I scoured the bookstores, but salespeople assumed I was looking for a humorous book. Even so, funny or serious, there was hardly anything published on the subject. In the psychology literature, I found only one journal article, written In German, in 1913, and several paragraphs on the subject in a few books.

I learned that newspapers in Japan have daily columns specifically devoted to discussions of in-law problems. I was convinced that in-law problems are just as prevalent here, though not discussed openly.

At one time, people were unwilling to talk about such subjects as sex, aging, and death. But now these subjects are openly discussed and written about. Perhaps people are still reluctant to discuss the problems they may be having with their in-laws. Instead, they may make jokes about their in-laws, disguising their painful feelings, or write anonymous letters to advice columnists.

I continued to find out more about in-law relationships. I interviewed more than 250 men and women of different ages, economic groups, and ethnic backgrounds, including American, Arab, Armenian, Bahamian, Dutch, Ethiopian, Greek, Irish, Israeli, Italian, Mexican, Polish, Russian, and Swedish. Despite all of their cultural differences, the in-law tensions were very similar.

This book illustrates the range of common in-law tensions by letting the interviewees speak for themselves. Their quotations show that each family has to find its own workable solutions. There is no one right way to feel or behave when we become in-laws.

The results of my interviews led me to conclude that becoming an in-law usually causes in everyone concerned — parents, children, siblings, parents-in-law, children-in-law, and siblings-in-law — normal, temporary tensions and disruptive feelings.

If you bought this book, I presume that you want to: (1) alleviate tensions with your in-laws or prospective in-laws; or (2) want to prevent such tensions. Whether you are an experienced in-law, or about to become one, I hope that reading about the wide diversity of feelings and experiences regarding in-law problems will be useful.

Scientists, especially physicists, have come to see that physical shapes and surfaces are not perfectly smooth, round, or straight, but rather are rough, irregular, and tangled. Analogously, in-law relationships also are not smooth and harmonious but rather complex and tangled. They may best be described in terms of individual episodes in people's lives — vignettes, filled with feelings, that describe how people grow and change, how in-laws separate and yet become close again.

It should be comforting to know that tensions are universally present to some degree in every in-law relationship and that you are not alone in wanting to know more about the subject. I hope that what I have found and described in this book will be of help to you, whether you are just entering or have already entered the tension-filled yet often supportive world of in-law relationships.

You are likely to learn more by trusting first impressions than by trying to look behind them.

HEINZ KOHUT,
20th-century psychoanalyst and author

CHAPTER

I

First Impressions

The Child-In-Law's Viewpoint

- ♦ *The First Meeting: the Young Couple's Perspective*
- ♦ *You Only Get One Chance to Make a Good First Impression*
- ♦ *Do your Homework Before you Meet your In-Laws*

You've most likely been told about the importance of making a good impression when interviewing for a job or college. Many books are available which prescribe what to wear and what to do on these occasions. But for that important first meeting with the parents of your fiance, there are no guidelines.

The first encounter between prospective in-laws is not a formal meeting between strangers, nor is it a casual meeting of new acquaintances. It is a meeting of people who will be inextricably bound up in each other's lives.

In most social situations, the first impression often influences whether or not you will pursue a relationship with a new person. Parents-in-law, however, come with the territory — they belong to the mate you have chosen, and there is no choice in the matter. As this newspaper photographer pointed out:

Not only are in-laws there, but they have all these rights. It's a big package that comes with them. They're there, and I'll have to buy them birthday presents.

3

As a prospective bride or groom, you are probably very concerned about making a good impression on your future in-laws. Psychoanalyst Heinz Kohut pointed out that under normal circumstances all humans need a steady stream of self-confirmation. Therefore, most people want to make a positive impression on their future-in-laws. One young woman expressed an almost universal desire:

> When I went to meet his parents, I dressed nicely because I wanted to make a good impression — they don't know you as a person yet.

Many young people feel anxiety about the first encounter. One man who felt unsure said:

> When I met my parents-in-law, I was shy. I didn't know what to think or say. I guess I was overwhelmed this whole situation.

Another young man vividly described his first meeting:

> The first time I visited, her mother came out with plates of cookies and fruit and introduced herself. I think it was the same the second time as well. The third time, the cookies and cake stopped, no more fruit, no more anything. She just kept an eye on me, watching what I was doing with her daughter. And from then on, it was an adversary type of relationship.

Besides the impression you make on the in-laws, also important is the impression that they make on you. First impressions of the prospective in-laws begin even before one meets them. The information and data acquired earlier help set the scene. A young journalist about to be engaged said, "I heard about his family for a whole year before I met them; when he met my family it was the same thing."

Having known the future in-laws previously can make things more pleasant. A woman married 18 years said:

> His mother used to sit behind us in the synagogue, so she knew me and was happy about me. There was no tension about who I was

and what kind of family I came from. I felt very comfortable with his parents. From the beginning it was a haven to be there.

Another woman felt that her relationship with her husband was better because their families had known each other for a long time:

I knew his parents two years. He knew my parents years and years. He knew what he was getting into. My husband and I have identical backgrounds. Our parents are the same age, and have the same economic status, not much difference in education, the same conservative background. Neither of us is spendthrifts. We seem to want the same things.

Negative information about the future in-laws can also influence the first impression. One woman said:

Before I married, I needed to be honest and to share everything with my husband-to-be about what kind of family I came from. My mother is neurotic, and my father is walking psychotic. I think it influenced my husband when he was with them. He had negativity because I did.

The first impression may be so positive that one becomes eager to become part of the family. One woman explained:

My mother-in-law was very gracious. I thought, 'What an ideal life.' I wanted that family. At first, I was not aware of all that was going on, and I learned later that every family has quirks and faults.

Another woman, married 25 years, instantly liked her mother-in-law:

I fell in love with her at first sight. She was the kind of woman I would have liked to have as a mother. She was very smart and very pretty. When I met her she was mature, had warmth, and was able to give to me without making demands. She had a funny way of saying nice things. I have dimples in my shoulders, and she'd say, 'All this and dimples, too.'

One woman was attracted to her parents-in-law because they were different from her parents:

> The thing that fascinated me about my in-laws was they were more emotionally alive than my parents. I saw them rant and rave and drink themselves into oblivion. I come from a reserved, socially correct upbringing on the North Shore where you don't let your emotions show. You did things in the proper manner. You wrote thank-you notes for this and for that.

First impressions may be indelible and affect your attitude toward the in-laws throughout a lifetime. A womandescribed her intense 30-year memory:

> My mother-in-law was glamorous. I was a small town girl by comparison. I was so awed by her. I tried to impress her. She was not thrilled with me, I was not thrilled with her. To this day I still have difficulty warming up to her.

Some people insist upon meeting the in-laws before becoming engaged. An Armenian-American went to visit his girlfriend's parents to purposely observe them before deciding whether to marry her:

> I wanted to see how her parents raised her. I knew if her parents brought her up right, she would bring my children up right. The way her parents raised her met with my approval. I knew if I married this woman, things that were instilled in her would be instilled in my kids.

Some people, both men and women, reported being determined to like their future parents-in-law, no matter what their first impression, because they were their mate's parents. This woman accepted her in-laws even though their household was different from her clean Polish home:

> I decided I was going to like them because I was madly in love, but they were different from my family. They seemed kind of slovenly. They were Shanty Irish with 12 kids in the family. They

thought nothing of writing phone numbers all over the walls. Everybody just took a pencil and wrote all over the walls in the kitchen. The dog made all over the floor, and everybody walked around it.

This man, too, was determined to like his father-in-law:

When I first met my father-in-law, I thought he was nuts. But since he was going to be my father-in-law, I said, 'Well, this is the man I have to love and try to like.'

Despite the immediate aversion this woman felt to her mother-in-law, she attempted to build a relationship:

When I met her, I was turned off. She was grossly overweight. She looked tailored with beautiful hair and nails. But without that, she is very coarse and vulgar. She swears in public, and just seems very crude. I told my husband, 'If I met your Mom at work, she is the kind of person that would not be my friend. But she is your mother, and I'm going to make the best of this relationship.'

We can't always be sure that our first impressions are correct. For some people it takes a long time to validate their feelings. Sometimes, first impressions prove false and have to be revised later. This man, married 13 years, admitted that he missed the mark completely in evaluating his in-laws:

I did not judge my father-in-law accurately. I thought my mother-in-law ran the show, when my father-in-law really runs the show. He is the first feature, the second feature, and the short subject.

Other people described the beginning of their relationship with their in-laws as filled with ambivalence. This woman was suspicious of her future mother-in-law's intentions:

My earliest memory of my mother-in-law is kind of a classic. I met her at a wedding, where she took me aside andtalked to me about how she thought my future husband had a lot of problems and she hoped I was really seriously considering what I was getting myself into. I remember thinking at the time that it reminded me of stories I had heard of mothers trying to talk future daughters-in-law out of marrying their sons.

Some people pay little heed to first impressions. A man married 30 years said this about his first meting with his future parents-in-law:

I'd say you really don't pay too much attention the first time you meet them. You see them, and there hasn't been too much communication. You know very little about them. It's a little too early for an impression.

Another man said:

First impressions are very important, but they should not be controlling or decisive because those who are making the impressions are putting their best foot forward.

No matter whether your first impressions are accurate or inaccurate, positive or negative, they are important. Often they can set the tone for the lifetime of the relationship.

SUGGESTIONS

The knowledge that you are about to meet your future in-laws could be an exciting, unnerving and tension-producing situation. Your future in-laws are probably experiencing similar feelings, for you will be evaluating them just as they will be evaluating you. This knowledge should help ease your tension.

A great deal depends on that first meeting, since it may very well set the tone and pattern for your future relationship. However, there is little more you can do to prepare for it except to dress appropriately and to put yourself in the right frame of mind. Don't hesitate to ask your fiancé questions about your prospective in-laws or to show an interest in their likes, dislikes, hopes and aspirations. The added knowledge will help you avoid the risk of offending them.

The Truth, the whole truth and nothing but the truth.

Portion of oath administered in court

CHAPTER

II

The Third Degree

The Parent-In-Law's Viewpoint

- ♦ *The First Meeting: the Parent-in-Law's Perspective*
- ♦ *Getting to Know You: Questions You May or Should Ask*
- ♦ *Never Underestimate the Importance of Good Manners*

During their courtship, couples usually have time to get to know each other. Parents, however, do not have a similar opportunity to get to know the prospective child-in-law. As a consequence, parents have many questions, doubts and fears about their child's choice of mate.

The questioning can begin before the first meeting, when the parents ask their child, "Whom are you dating?" Some parents may voice their apprehensions early. One woman in this study reported:

My daughter said she met a fellow. I asked, 'What does he do?'
'He's an entertainer,' she answered. I said, 'Do you realize what you're doing, what kind of lifestyle you're letting yourself in for?'

At the first meeting, although the parents may not question the prospective child-in-law in a formal manner, many questions run through their minds. In reality they would like to give the newcomer the third degree: What do you do? Can you support my child? What kind of family are you from? What do your parents do? Are you good enough for my child? What kind of genes will my grandchildren inherit from you? Will you make my child happy?

Some of these questions will actually be asked while others are questions the parents cannot ask. One father-in-law reported asking directly, "Tell me, what are your plans? How will you support my daughter?"

Some questions may be answered easily, others may be more difficult, and some can't be answered at all. For example: "Is my future son-in-law a giving or understanding person?" One married woman said, "You don't really find out about a person until you live with him."

When the child-in-law comes from a great distance, there is little opportunity for the in-law relationship to develop before the marriage. One father described the beginning of his relationship with his son-in-law:

> The real beginning comes when I weighed all of the factors, and was able to form an opinion. At first, we didn't get to know him because our daughter moved away. Only after their engagement did we learn more about him and his capabilities. Then we asked people about his parents. He comes from a respectable family; they are considered strange, but they haven't caused any scandal.

Despite any prior information they may have about the children-in-law, parents are often apprehensive about the wisdom of their child's choice. As one parent said:

> He talked to us on the phone. He sounds good and fine and hardworking and wants to meet us. He comes from a very close and caring family. But his mother still does his laundry. Even as my daughter wastelling me this, my reaction was to be protective of her. I said, 'If you think it's unhealthy and his mother is too strong, talk to him about it.'

We all have ideals and values that we would like to see passed on to the next generation. The "third degree" is an attempt to determine how we think the prospective child-in-law reflects those values.

It is easier to be accepting if the child-in-law lives up to our standards. One woman was pleased with her son's choice because she saw her own values reflected in his bride:

The distinguishing thing about my daughter-in-law was that she was sensitive to people around her, yet she did not placate us or fawn on us. You could see she had breeding, not blue-blood, but she had a sense of courtesy that was not just surface. You could see she was good for him, he was so happy around her.

This man was pleased that his son-in-law lived up to his expectations:

If I had to find somebody to fit a job description for a son-in-law, mine would fit the bill completely. He's steady, reliable, honest, a hard-working guy, and he has many of the traits that we've lost in life, like initiative.

However, when the desired characteristics do not appear in their child-in-law, parents are disappointed. One woman said about her new daughter-in-law, "She's nothing like what I expected him to marry." This father-in-law was quite emphatic in voicing his disapproval:

My son-in-law was a real schmuck, and I couldn't wait for my daughter to get divorced. He was from a farm in Vermont. She was from Beverly Hills. He did not have street smarts. He was a low-key guy, and the nature of her business was such that she was meeting a lot of sharp guys. He looked bad compared to the others who were well-dressed, well-mannered.

Even if parents disapprove of the child-in-law, they are helpless because the choice is not theirs to make. One father said:

The guy was 6'4". He weighed about 300 pounds. I said to her, 'What is this?' And the first thing she said was, 'Daddy, I'm old enough to know what I'm doing. I'm going to marry him whether you like him or not.' I disliked the man intensely, but what could I do? They were married.

Other parents accept whomever their child chooses, even if they don't feel 100 percent acceptance and approval for the future child-in-law. One father reported:

My first impressions were sort of guarded, with the thought in mind that this is who my child wants to marry. I must do what I can to accept the child's spouse. This does not mean to say things aren't noticed that you would like to have different.

And of course, some parents wholeheartedly approve of their child's choice, as did this father:

I said to my daughter, 'If you like him and he likes you, hold on to him. He's a good boy.'

Unless parents are psychologically disturbed, they usually do not want to hold on to their children forever. They would like to see their children form meaningful and loving relationships which would result in a transmission of values and ideals to the coming generation. The "third degree" can be a natural and healthy attempt to determine the willingness of their prospective child-in-law to respect and to transmit these values and ideals.

SUGGESTIONS

When you first meet the newest most important person in your child's present and future, his mate-to-be, you will undoubtedly feel excited and tense. But realize that you are not alone in that respect. The prospective child-in-law will be just as excited and tense as you are, if not more. Try to imagine his feelings. No matter how self-assured and self-confident he1 may appear, he would like your approval. It is up to you, as an experienced parent, to be a bit more understanding of him than he may be of you.

It is only natural for you to want to know all about him. Don't be afraid to ask such questions as what he does, what his background is, what his plans are. But realize that the manner and tone in which these questions are asked are as important as the questions.

Treat your prospective child-in-law with the same respect and interest that you would like from him. This will help get your relationship off to a good start.

WHAT IF YOU DISAPPROVE?

Even if you approve of your future child-in-law's background, there is no guarantee that you will like him. The most important thing is that your child and his future mate like and respect each other. Nevertheless, what if you disapprove of the match?

If you are dissatisfied with your child's choice, try to figure out why. Are you confusing your unmet needs with those of your child? Discuss your concerns with your child, spouse, friends, or perhaps, a therapist. You may need to discuss the matter thoroughly before you can "step back" and see your child as a capable adult who can take care of his own needs. By the time your child has made a decision to marry a particular person, it probably is too late for you to influence his decision. Even if your child's choice disappoints you, the choice ultimately is your child's.

If you strongly disapprove of your child's choice, explain your objections early and in a rational manner. Discuss the pros and cons of the marriage. But listen to your child's viewpoint too. After all, unless your child is under age, the decision is his. If he makes a poor choice, he is responsible for the consequences.

If your child goes ahead with the marriage despite your disapproval, try to maintain a relationship with him. Because the emotional ties between you and your child continue throughout life, communication between you should also continue.

IT TAKES TIME TO BUILD
A RELATIONSHIP

Realize that although the couple get to know each other before they get engaged, you and the child-in-law will probably start the in-law relationship essentially as strangers.

Just as it takes time for the married couple's relationship to develop and solidify, so, too, will it take time for you and your child-in-law to grow to accept, trust, and feel comfortable with each other.

Realize that you can do only so much to make the future child-in-law comfortable. For the in-law relationship to work, the child-in-law has to do his share too. You cannot demand or impose closeness. It takes willingness and patience on both sides to build a close, trusting in-law relationship. But the rewards are worth the effort.

In the meantime, broaden the scope of your social network: make new friends, develop new interests, dothings that make you feel worthwhile. Having good friends and satisfying activities will enable you to feel better and thereby be more understanding of your child-in-law.

If you have a lot of trouble doing this, a psychotherapist may be able to help.

And they lived happily ever after.

THE BROTHERS GRIMM

III

Looking For Something Missing

- ♦ *Surprise, In-Laws Offer Unexpected Benefits*
- ♦ *Wishful Thinking About Your In-Laws may be Just That*
- ♦ *Tame Your Fantasies and Expectations*

A concomitant benefit of marriage could be discovering in your spouse's family something that was lacking in your own family. Though this seems to happen by chance, the choice of a spouse may have been precipitated by this need. Many people have found the warmth, attention, closeness, excitement, stability and freedom from financial worries that were missing during their single years.

Some people may enter into a marriage in order to satisfy specific needs. One man who had lost his parents at an early age looked at marriage as a vehicle for acquiring a family. Others who seek family connections and wealth expressed themselves as did one man: "I was looking for in-laws who were extremely wealthy and generous."

One woman was quite explicit in what she wanted:

When I first got married, I was not close to my mother. She certainly was not what I wanted to be. I wanted to be an elegant North Shore matron. My mother-in-law fit the bill. She was perfect, educated, and socially cultured, everything I wanted. I

19

just glommed onto her, and she was delighted to have me do so because she only had sons. I just thought she was wonderful. I was the student, and she was the teacher.

In this instance, the mother-in-law, too, found something that had been missing in her life — a daughter she could cultivate.

As one matures, the needs and perceptions change. An idealized parent-in-law may disappoint the child-in-law by revealing imperfections. In the above case, the daughter-in-law became disenchanted when she noted that her mother-in-law was very generous and warm to members of her family but very stingy and arrogant toward others.

Nonetheless, it is important to note that in-laws often do help fill an emotional void for the child-in-law. This woman found the extended family she had lacked:

I came from a difficult family. I was an only child. My mother was mentally ill. She didn't want me home. I came into my mother-in-law's household infatuated and fascinated because it seemed to me like a large, extended family. There were grandparents and all these relatives. There were a lot of young people around because there were lots of cousins. I thought it was great.

One woman told how her family provided the warmth and nurturing that was missing in her husband's family:

My husband's family never wished each other a 'Happy Birthday.' When it was one of their birthdays, everyone went his own way. They never had any family dinners. They did not celebrate the holidays. These things were not meaningful to them. With my side of the family, it is very important to be together. We do not have to love each other, and we do not have to see each other all the time. But we always want it to be so that we could speak and be able to get together for the holidays or the kids' birthdays.

She also described how different her husband's mother was from her own:

My mother-in-law couldn't give on any level whatsoever. I truly don't think that this woman had the capacity of really caring about anyone but herself. Jim adores my mother. My mother always gives him a birthday card that says, 'To my wonderful son!' She brings candy and little gifts to him. He found in my family something he never had in his.

Some people find what they need for their emotional growth. One woman said she learned from her parents-in-law how to talk more freely about emotions: "In our family, we didn't express feelings. Since I'm married, I'm getting better about expressing them."

Another woman found her spouse's family appealing because they related to each other so differently from her own family:

I'll never forget when I first went to visit my husband's family as a high school kid. I sat down at the table with him and his brother. The two of them teased their mother about how fat she was. I almost fell under the table with absolute embarrassment. I couldn't believe my ears that anybody would do that and she could take it in such good spirits and tease them back. This was something so foreign and yet, in their family, one of the most attractive features. When we left I said, 'How could you do that to your mother?' He said, 'Well, we've always learned to say what we think about everything.'

This was in sharp contrast to the way she grew up:

I grew up in a very inhibitive atmosphere. 'Don't say that to your sister, because you're going to hurt her feelings and upset her.' 'You may feel that way, but don't get her upset' or 'Don't ruffle anybody's feelings.'

However, sometimes those yearning for something missing are frustrated rather than fulfilled by their in-laws. One woman described her unsatisfied wish that her in-laws would be like parents to her. Her mother had died when she was 14, her father when she was 18. She had just moved to Chicago when she met her husband.

It took 20 years of marriage to accept that her wishes would not come true:

> I was looking more for a set of parents than in-laws. My expectation was more than they could ever produce because they were not looking for another child. They had five children. I was 22 and starry-eyed about getting a new set of parents. Plus, I was in Chicago by myself, no family, no friends. I didn't know anyone. I think that contributed to my expectation of his family being more than a set of in-laws.

Newlyweds begin their marriage with the hope that they will live happily ever after — having a good relationship with both their spouse and their spouse's family. Just as plants naturally grow toward the sun, so, too, do human beings have a natural tendency to seek out those people who will satisfy their needs. If they are lucky, they will receive from their in-law family the understanding, affirmation, and encouragement that they seek.

SUGGESTIONS FOR CHILDREN-IN-LAW

Your wish to be liked and accepted by your in-laws is very natural. But to expect your in-laws to treat you with excessive admiration or generosity may stem from current or old unmet needs. No one can undo your past or make up to you what was missing in your childhood. Knowing this may help you tone down your excessive expectations. In some cases, you may need the help of a psychotherapist to tame these needs.

Your need for respect is similar to theirs. If you are respectful and polite to your in-laws, the chances are better that they will respond in kind.

SUGGESTIONS FOR PARENTS-IN-LAW

To hope that your child-in-law will be a fine person who will make your child happy is quite natural. But you may have some unrealistic fantasies and expectations about whom your child will marry. Or you may even feel that your child's marriage is a second chance to fulfill your dreams. For example, if you never had a son, you may expect your son-in-law to be as close to you as your own son might have been. Or you may envision that your new daughter-in-law will be a better daughter to you than the one you have now. You may have an unreasonable need to be adored and appreciated for whatever you do.

You should be aware that your child and child-in-law must satisfy each other's needs, not yours, as they begin their life together. Your needs must be satisfied elsewhere. Respect and politeness are the most that you ought to expect. Anything over and above that is gravy.

*Recently we passed through a period in my house
during which an unusually large amount
of glass was broken; I myself was responsible for
some of the damage but the little psychical epidemic
could easily be explained; these were the days
before my eldest daughter's wedding.*

SIGMUND FREUD,
Standard Edition, Vol. 6, 1901, p. 173

CHAPTER
IV

Whose Wedding Is It, Anyway?

⧫ *Before the Wedding: Excitement and Trepidation*
⧫ *Who Pays for What and Other Worries*
⧫ *The Wedding Ceremony: a Grand Finale and a Fresh Start*

Weddings, with their gowns, tuxedos, flowers, food, music and dancing, are supposed to be joyous occasions. People look forward to them. Yet, almost inevitably, those intimately involved feel stress at these times. How ironic it is that this hopeful ceremony for the newlyweds can cause tension and frustration.

In the midst of making wedding plans, family members may be surprised to find themselves shouting or even screaming at each other. One woman said that planning her daughter's wedding was a nightmare. Another divorced woman whose daughter was about to marry said, "It's a terrible time. I just stayed out of it and paid the bills." Old wishes and insecurities resurface as everyone tries to plan the perfect wedding. Relatives may often tug at the young couple with unreasonable demands. One grandmother, for example, asked the bride and groom to change their wedding date because it conflicted with her vacation.

A wedding is a transition in the lives of all those involved, and at any transition strong feelings are stirred up. Each person may feel excitement and anticipation, as well as trepidation. The young couple hope for a bright future, yet may be apprehensive and unsure

27

about what that future holds. The parents may feel a sense of loss commingled with their joy. In addition, the parents may recall old unresolved feelings of disappointment and may view the wedding as an opportunity to rectify these old hurts and disappointments. This may account for their emphasis on what they want at the wedding, not necessarily what the bride and groom want.

The wedding is ostensibly for the bride and groom, but the two sets of parents and siblings often make self-serving suggestions and even unreasonable demands. The blend of all the participants' wishes and expectations can affect the amount of stress produced. Though not inevitable, it is likely that there will be strains and stresses.

Parents and other family members can begin to exert pressures on a young couple even before the engagement. Family influences on a young couple's decisions may begin as early as the choosing of engagement rings. One woman said:

> When I got engaged, I couldn't get the kind of ring I wanted because I had to get the kind the cousins gave their wives. I wanted an emerald-shaped diamond, and I got a pear shape. I got a beautiful ring, but I didn't want it — which wasn't the way you start out a marriage.

Another woman told about her family's tradition not to have engagement rings: "My mother didn't have one, I didn't have one, and my daughter-in-law never had one."

Some young couples stand up to their parents' pressure but may feel regretful later. One woman said:

> My mother wanted to come and choose the ring with us. We said no. In retrospect, I should have let her. I would have ended up with a much bigger diamond.

Disagreements over wedding plans can stir up stress and lead to irritations. Some parents feel that it is their prerogative to plan the wedding and have things their way. An older bride was annoyed by her in-laws' demands:

Here I was, 33, and my in-laws were telling me how to plan my wedding, and which caterer to use. I was amazed. I had been planning and handling things for myself for so long, and here they wanted me to use another caterer.

This man, married one year, said:

Let's not kid ourselves, the wedding is for the parents. I would have been happy with five or ten people at my wedding. But her parents wanted to invite a lot of people, and my parents wanted a gigantic wedding in the grand ballroom. So for them, our wedding was not lavish enough, not big enough.

One bride's mother said with great seriousness and no humor:

I am convinced that if the parents paid for it, it's really the mother's wedding. The daughter just comes along for the ride. She'll have her turn when her daughter gets married. I felt the wedding was my production rather than my daughter's, and she was aware of that.

Some couples fight in what may seem to be an underhanded manner — yet with humor — for what they want at their wedding. One man described his on-going struggle with his prospective mother-in-law:

If we had to do it over again, we would never go through with it. My mother-in-law really made it miserable. It was one thing after another — the music, the flowers, the photographer, who is going to eat, and how many people. I knew that if I wanted to invite ten people, it would be too many. So I figured that what I had to do was pad the list a little. Jimmy Carter was invited, Ronald Reagan was invited. I padded it a little bit here and a little bit there. When she saw the total number of people I invited, she said, 'You will have to pay for it yourselves.' And so I said very pensively, 'Well, okay, Ronald Reagan, we're not all that good friends, we will knock him off.' I trimmed that list down a little bit, yet I got everybody I wanted.

Others stand up to the parents more directly, as did this bride:

My first really big fight with my mother-in-law was about the wedding. She seemed to be very upset about what color I chose. I perceived this as her wanting to make it her wedding and not allowing me to plan my wedding. I was trying to decide between pink and lilac. It turns out she had very morbid associations with both colors. First, she was trying to talk me out of pink, and then I said, 'Well, lilac was really my favorite, anyway.' Then she was trying to talk me out of lilac and back to pink. So I ended up screaming at her on the phone. I had to assert my independence. I asserted myself, she backed away, and that was it.

The expense of the wedding is an important consideration and is often a source of conflict between the families involved. How much money is available and how people feel about it and themselves when spending it become critical issues. Some parents will amiably negotiate the amount of money that will be spent, and who will pay for what. But others do not feel that they were heard, or that their negotiations were successful.

One bride's father described his negotiations about the wedding expenses:

I know a lot of couples will split according to who could afford what. But my son-in-law and his father absolutely disagreed with me. They wouldn't budge. We ended up with a traditional pattern of the bride's parents paying for nearly everything.

In this case the resentment and animosity that was stirred up between the bride's and the groom's parents lasted many years.

Another groom described his father-in-law's vacillations about spending money for his stepdaughter's wedding:

One day my father-in-law said he's not going to pay for anything. Then he said he's going to pay for some things. It turned out that my wife and I paid for most of the wedding, but her father took all the credit. Now he will tell you, 'I made you a gorgeous wedding.'

Other parents spend money freely despite feeling apprehensive about the possibility of wasting money on an unsuccessful marriage. One father said, 'You know, I'm paying for this wedding but I feel like I'm throwing money down the toilet. This marriage can't last.' Another mother told the newlyweds they had to stay married at least twelve years in order to pay for the wedding.

Some parents spend more than they can afford in order to impress their friends and neighbors. A groom's mother complained about her daughter-in-law's parents:

> People try to do things at a wedding they cannot afford. You ought to do what you are capable of, whether they are the parents of the son or of the daughter. My daughter-in-law's parents had no money. But they tired to put on a wedding like they were millionaires.

Other parents are more practical about their limited funds. One father explained:

> You'd like to be a big sport, but it isn't all that easy. There's a reality of how much money there is. You have to make the most of what you have.

Some parents are willing to spend any amount of money to avoid conflict. One mother said:

> If it can be solved by money, then let it. You smile and say yes to anything. The wedding is such a provoking time, but it's only three hours. Whatever they want, fine and good, do it.

Planning the wedding celebration arouses a host of tensions not only between parents and children-in-law, but also between parents and their own children. A bride said:

> Two days before my wedding, my mother didn't want me to marry my husband. She was crying and didn't want to talk. Then she calmed down. When we had the rehearsal dinner, she became mad at his family forsome reason. Then the day of the wedding,

his mother walked in and didn't say hello to me. Everybody had a time to be angry. First, my mom, then me, then his mother. I was worried about what as going to happen the next night at the wedding because everybody was so mad at each other.

A mother described her son's irritation with her:

I know everyone is supposed to be tense during the wedding, especially mothers-in-law. During the picture taking, I was thinking my daughter-in-law's dress wasn't going to show in the picture, so I said to her, 'Hold your flowers lower.' She started to lower her flowers, but my son turned around and said to me in a very critical voice, 'Don't tell my wife how to hold her flowers, she knows how to hold her flowers.'

However, many reported that the weddings ran smoothly and left happy memories, at least partly because of the understanding and help given by the parents and parents-in-law. One mother said:

I think the wedding was for the bride and groom. They did everything. I gave advice on the biggies. I did it to facilitate the acquisition of a dress, for example. I made the suggestions, but they made the choices. I made all the contacts, and the wedding was not tense at all.

This daughter-in-law appreciated her prospective mother-in-law's understanding:

During the time we were planning the wedding, I didn't see much of my mother-in-law because we lived a long distance away. A lot of communication was through my husband. I was not aware of her need to be communicated with, and she was not pushing. I was not trying to keep in touch, yet whenever there was contact as the wedding drew close, she gave me the feeling of 'Don't worry about me. I'm here to help you,' which was lovely.

Some women even sewed the wedding gowns for their daughters-in-law. Others arranged the entire wedding for them. A woman recalled the wedding her mother-in-law planned:

The wedding was overwhelming. There were about 300 people there, it was very elaborate, and I felt like I was a guest, which I really was. My mother-in-law had made all the arrangements. I came from out of town, so it was all done here. She chose the flowers, everything. There wasn't mother-in-law tension at all. She has good taste. It was lovely. I didn't come from a lot of money. I couldn't possibly feel comfortable making those kinds of decisions, especially when I wasn't paying for it. I felt grateful that she was taking care of all of it.

We see that there are many different ways of planning a wedding and dividing up the wedding costs, depending on the parents' finances and their attitudes about spending.

Nevertheless, even with consideration and understanding from others, the bride and groom may be undergoing their own inner stress and anxieties about the impending change in their way of life. This may be reflected for example, in weight gain or loss. One bride said:

I gained weight with the problems I was having during the engagement. Before the wedding, I lost the weight, and four times they cut the gown down, from a size 16 to a size 12. The tailor refused to touch it anymore. He said it was a good thing I was getting married already.

A young bride described the various pressures she felt as she tried to please her parents, her friends, and herself:

Mine was the first wedding in the family. It was all maids of honor with the same dresses, a real traditional wedding. Everything and everyone was involved. All my girlfriends were right there waiting for their bridesmaid dresses. I had to take time to go shopping with them and match them in identical dresses. I had to do all this, plus working and school.

An important area of concern is the clothing worn by members of the wedding party. This emphasis on clothes may reflect a normal, healthy need to look good. But an overemphasis on what is worn, at one extreme, or a complete disregard of the importance of looking good, at the other extreme, can reflect inner turmoil and even resistance to participate in the wedding. One bride became very angry as she described her mother-in-law's appearance at her formal church wedding:

> My mother-in-law showed up at our wedding wearing a wrinkled dress she had worn for her other son's wedding. She could have worn something else a little bit nicer, and not a repeat of her other son's wedding. That deeply offended me and my parents.

Another woman described her father-in-law's stubbornness before the wedding:

> Up to the day of our marriage, my father-in-law wasn't going to walk down the aisle. My husband got the tuxedo and sized it up from another suit. Only at the very last minute did my father-in-law decide to walk down the aisle wearing the tuxedo. He just absolutely didn't want my husband to get married at such an early age.

A wedding heralds the end of one era and the beginning of another for all participants. Parents may feel concern about the possible loss of affection from their children. One mother stated:

> Things ran into a depression after the wedding. I really don't know why. Perhaps you are feeling a sense of loss — these are feelings you try to submerge.

Some parents reported intense feelings of loss when the youngest child married. A woman explained: 'With my youngest child things were easier. I felt more satisfied in parenting him than I did with the others. My feelings of loss became more acute when he got married.' One young man understood his mother's feelings about marrying off her youngest son:

> This is a transition period. Not only is it giving away a child, but it's giving away a whole stage of life. My mother was a lot older, I am the youngest, and she'd given away before, but she had a hard time giving me away.

Guests are invited to the wedding to share in the joy of the occasion, but they perform another important function. Their presence gives emotional support to the family as the old relationships shift to make room for the new ones that are being developed.

The tact, consideration, compromise and diplomacy shown during the planning stages will have a definite impact on those relationships.

SUGGESTIONS FOR THE BRIDE AND GROOM

I repeat once more: each of us needs to feel important and appreciated. These feelings are usually fostered when people are treated with politeness and respect.

This is your wedding. If you have strong convictions and wishes about what you want, respectfully say so. If not, your parents may have a say, especially if they are paying for the wedding.

No matter who pays for the wedding, the couple ought to discuss, decide, and assert what they want: the time, the place, the guest list, the music, the color scheme, etc. If the couple pays for all the arrangements, they may have things exactly as they wish. But if they turn to parents for financial assistance, they should be prepared to compromise some of their wishes.

SUGGESTIONS FOR THE PARENTS

Remember that it is your child's and prospective child-in-law's marriage celebration, as well as yours. Be there to help your adult children carry out their ideas and plans. Also, do not forget to consider the wishes and needs of the other set of parents.

SUGGESTIONS FOR ALL INVOLVED

Be aware that there will be frustrations no matter how well you planned the wedding, and that many of these frustrations are natural reactions to this important change in your lives.

Good luck, smile, and enjoy the wedding.

*No word arouses more awe and dread amongst
primitive people than the word mother-in-law.*

SIR JAMES GEORGE FRAZER,
***19th-century anthropologist,
author of "The Golden Bough"***

Don't Call Me Mom

- *Two Emotionally Packed Words in any Language:*
  Mom and Dad
- *Is it Disloyal to Call your Father-in-Law, Dad?*
- *Bite the Bullet: Discuss What to Call your In-Laws*

No two words in the English language arouse more emotion than the terms a person uses to address his parents (e.g., "Mom" and "Dad" or "Mother" and "Father"). Because of their strong positive (or negative) connotation it can become difficult for us to address another person by those names. Consequently, problems may arise as to how we are to address our-in-laws.

Some European-born Jews in this country address their parents-in-law by the Yiddish words shviger and shver, meaning "mother-in-law" and "father-in-law," respectively. Others, however, consider these terms pejorative, just as some people consider the words "mother-in-law" and "father-in-law" derogatory. In our culture, there are not set rules or formulas for determining how to address a parent-in-law.

Anthropologist Sir James Frazer pointed out in his book, The Golden Bough, that some primitive cultures have strict rules about names. Among the New Guinean Sea Dyaks, for example, people related to each other by marriage are forbidden to pronounce each other's names. They believe that a man will bring on the wrath of evil spirits if he pronounces the name of his father-in-law or mother-in-law. Among the African Caffres, a woman is forbidden to pronounce the name of her father-in-law, and a man to pronounce the name of his mother-in-law.

I asked the participants in this study what they called their in-laws, and how they chose those names. The replies revealed the discomfort that many felt in deciding how to address their parents-in-law. A female lawyer said:

> I never thought I would call my in-laws 'Mom and Dad.' I never wanted to, and I never did to their faces. I never called them anything for about two and one-half years! It was amazing how skillfully I avoided using any names. If I was on the telephone speaking to one in-law and I wanted to speak to the other, rather than use the word 'Mom' or 'Dad' I'd just hang up and try another time. My husband told me to start calling them by their first names. He thought it was ridiculous that I wouldn't call them anything to the point where I would call them back on the phone just to get the person I wanted, or make him call so he could ask for the one I wanted to talk to.

One housewife said:

> I don't call them by name. I can't. It's just not in me to call them 'Mom' or 'Pop' or 'Mother' and 'Father.' I might refer to them as 'Your mother said this' or 'Your father said that' instead of 'Mom said' or 'Dad said.' My husband's the same, he won't call my parents 'Mom' or 'Dad.' He refers to them by their first names, but not to their faces.

A male lawyer stated:

> I think I might have used first names at the beginning, but as the relationship developed in closeness, it seemed to become more awkward to call them by their first names. Because of the awkwardness, you search for another name and find nothing. Then 'Mom' and 'Dad' come into place.

One woman said that she called her mother-in-law 'Mother' but felt that she would choke each time she said it. She would never dream of calling her by her first name. She went on to describe the various names which her own daughter-in-law uses for her:

> At first she called me 'Mrs. M.' Later she called me 'Mom M.' Now she calls me by my first name. I was offended at this. She is not my peer. She's not my generation. I'm not her friend. I hear the wavering and questioning in her voice when she calls me by my first name. I wish she would ask me what I'd like to be called.

This mother-in-law seemed to have more sympathy:

> She doesn't call me anything, and I find this very common. I think it's very difficult for the young people who have mothers to call their mother-in-law 'Mom.' At first I wanted to be called something. I didn't feel I was her girlfriend. I was her mother-in-law. But if she can't, she can't. It's not going to make me love her less — she makes my son happy, and she's given me a beautiful grandchild.

One woman thought it was a problem of self-confidence:

> Calling my mother-in-law 'Mother' was so difficult. Perhaps it depends on your age. You're terribly insecure in your own relationship at first. You don't know where you stand with your own mate. And before you establish any family feelings with strangers, you're cautious.

Some people do not discuss this issue with their spouse or with their in-laws. They simply decide for themselves which name to use, but this is not always acceptable to the in-law. A mother-in-law who liked her daughter-in-law nevertheless disliked her choice of name:

> It takes a certain amount of confidence to bring up this controversial subject and talk about it. I don't like my daughter-in-law to call me by my first name. I felt affronted by her calling me that in a letter. It was so revolting to me when she wrote and called me 'Dear Katherine.'

A person may have known his in-laws for many years before his engagement or marriage, but the new relationship seems to demand that he address them less formally than before. Yet there still may be great discomfort in deciding what to call them. One woman described her difficulty:

> I remember when I was engaged and I had to call my fiancÈ's mother on the phone. I had known her for seven years, so I had been calling them 'Mr.' and 'Mrs.' All of a sudden, overnight, I was supposed to start calling them 'Mom' and 'Dad.' I sat and looked at the phone for an hour. I agonized. I would dial half of the number. It was so weird, I just could not say, 'Hi, Mom.' They're not the type of people who would want me to call them by their first names, so that was out.

Some respondents had no conflicting feelings about calling the parents-in-law "Mom" or "Dad," saying that it felt natural to do so. Others felt that to address their parents-in-law in the same manner as they do their parents may even be a compliment to both sets of parents. A significant number, however, admitted that they felt disloyal to their own parents if they called others by the same names. The opportunity for the child-in-law to call the parent-in-law by a name such as "Grandma" or "Grandpa" may help improve in-law relationship.

Many people reported that they never called their parents-in-law anything until grandchildren were born, then called them "Grandma" and "Grandpa."

The problem of what to call a child-in-law and how to introduce him does not appear to be as sensitive a problem. Most people are comfortable calling their children-in-law by their first names, and most children-in-law do not mind. It is certainly more appropriate for a older person to call a younger person by his first name. Nevertheless, problems occasionally arise in being introduced. This lawyer reported her resentment at what she considered a charade played by her parents-in-law:

> Whenever I am introduced to some of their friends, they say, 'This is our daughter.' Since these are not close friends, but

acquaintances, they look a little puzzled because my in-laws only have sons. Then my father-in-law or mother-in-law says, 'She's really our daughter-in-law, she's married to our youngest son, but we feel so close to her that we think of her really as our daughter,' which I think is a very nice thing to say. But I don't want her to be my mother — I have a mother.

What people call each other may reflect expectations and desires. Such introductions as "This is my Dad" or "This is my son" may indicate a wish that the parent-in-law will be like a parent, perhaps even a better parent than one's own, or that the adult child-in-law will be like a child, the son or daughter one never had, or a better son or daughter. One man said:

> The words 'Mom' and 'Dad' mean a lot because it's a crucial relationship that has developed over time. But the in-law relationship is a new one without allegiances. To say 'Mother' or 'Father' to an in-law is just as intimate as using a first name. It's basically an aspiration and expectation that an in-law is supposed to be intimate.

Siblings and even spouses may feel jealous at hearing their parents addressed as "Mom" or "Dad" by the new child-in-law. This feeling may dissipate as the child-in-law becomes accepted as an integral part of the family.

Some parents may also feel disloyal to their children to be addressed as "Mom" and "Dad" by the child-in-law and may specifically request that the child-in-law call them by their first name. Some may also consider their child-in-law as their peer and would feel more comfortable on a first-name basis. People in second marriages may also feel more comfortable calling their new parents-in-law by their first names.

The question of what to call in-laws may become less important as time passes, as this woman pointed out:

> When Phil and I were married, it was just so disloyal to my own parent to call my mother-in-law 'Mom.' As the years go by, I think how foolish I was. Why did it bother me? She was really a very good woman. She'd do anything for me.

In my study, there seemed to be no correlation between what people called their in-laws and how they felt about them. They may call an in-law 'Mom' or 'Dad,' yet feel very artificial and distant doing so, or,conversely, they may address their in-laws as 'Mr.' and 'Mrs.,' yet care for them very much.

SUGGESTIONS

Although what one calls an in-law does not necessarily reflect the closeness of the relationship, it does involve sensitivities.

An early discussion of what in-laws should call each other would allow each person to air his feelings and would thus reduce stress and tension. Soon after a couple decides to marry, they should discuss with their future parents-in-law what to call each other.

Because parents-in-law probably experienced the same problem early in their marriage, it may be easier for them to raise the question by saying, 'What would you like to call me?' or 'This is what I prefer to be called,' or offer various choices. If the parents don't raise the issue, it is entirely appropriate for the children to do so. Addressing each other by mutually agreed-upon names is far better than avoiding the subject and maintaining an awkward situation.

And they went away and left me.

**Frankie, 12-year-old sister of the groom,
in "The Member of the Wedding"
by Carson McCullers**

CHAPTER
VI

Brothers- And Sisters-In-Law

- *Siblings "Left Behind" After the Wedding Want your Love*
- *Siblings Offer the Married Couple Physical and Emotional Help and Many Acts of Kindness*
- *Good Relationships are a Two-Way Street*

Developing positive relationships with siblings-in-law, regardless of their geographical proximity, can offer many benefits to a new bride or groom. However, it is important to keep in mind that these good relationships do not develop instantly, but in stages, just as other in-law relationships.

Before the marriage, brothers and sisters mirror the same unspoken questions and high standards that the parents do: 'Who is this person? Will he fit into the family? Will he be good to my brother or my sister? Will he like me? Will I like him? Is he really good enough for my brother or sister?

One teenager described his feelings about his sister's dates:

I never liked who she was dating. I always thought she could do better. I wouldn't let her go to the door if the guy was honking. I'd say, 'Wait until he comes to the door.'

This protective, as well as demanding attitude, does not immediately disappear when the date becomes a brother- or sister-in-law.

47

Many people, regardless of age, feel abandoned when a sibling marries, especially if they have had a strong attachment to that person. For example, in Carson McCullers' book, *The Member of The Wedding*, a young girl is devastated when she is not allowed to go along with her brother on his honeymoon. One woman in this study said:

> My brother and I were brought up close. It was hard to give him up. There's a fear that you are going to lose your brother and he won't love you as much as he did in the past.

One bride, who had not called her sister for four weeks after her wedding, received a tearful call from her sister, who said, 'I feel you don't love me anymore.'

Some people react to the disruption of their relationships with their sibling by being irritable, depressed, or even resentful of the sibling-in-law, as was as this 16-year-old:

> I was so close to my sister, but I felt alone after she married. So I made fun of anything my brother-in-law said.

In contrast, others became close to the new in-law, as did these women:

> I was in sixth grade when my older sister married. It seemed she was out so much that it didn't matter. I didn't feel I was losing her. I felt like I was getting a brother. He was the one who wrote me letters in camp, and he was the one who was better at being a brother than she was a sister.

> My brother-in-law was a positive, exciting thing in my life. There wasn't any disruption, only joy and happiness.

Some people are affected by what they see going on in the lives of their married siblings, as were these women:

> I never had any personal antipathy toward my brother-in-law, but my parents did. I was on the sideline not understanding, but I

knew he was making my sister unhappy. My brother-in-law is successful in the art world. People imitate and venerate him. But he is crazy. At first, it looked like my sister was having a great life with him. Their lives were exciting, artish, and experimental. I thought trying to develop yourself with experiences was the greatest idea until I saw the pain in their relationship. When I saw all the pain he caused, I became afraid of being experimental and free. I decided that I would have a different kind of life.

As the sibling-in-law relationship evolves, feelings may change, and warmth and closeness may develop. 'He grew on me,' said one young man, 'Once he showed he cared for my sister, there was something there.'

The new in-law may make overtures of friendship toward the siblings. Some siblings may welcome these overtures, which one woman described as 'a happy discovery of an ally.' However, some may not respond, as these people found:

I made a point of asking his sisters to be bridesmaids and had them over a few times. I made sure a lot of men were invited so they could meet them. But his sisters didn't call to talk. One didn't want to be a bridesmaid. They didn't offer to make me a shower. You can't go through life thinking everything is going to be reciprocated, but you'd like it to be.

I'm to the point where there's only so many times a person can hurt your feelings. The last three times we drove 300 miles to go visit my brother and sister-in-law. I asked, 'Why don't you drive down to see us?' and they answered, 'Cause we can't leave the bird and dog alone.' I'm just to the point where I don't care if I see my brother and sister-in-law anymore.

It takes effort to keep relationships close. One woman described how she and her sister-in-law would plan yearly vacations together so that their families, which lived far apart, could grow to know each other.

Another woman appreciated her sister-in-law's efforts to maintain closeness:

I don't think my brother, left alone, would remember whose birthday it was. My sister-in-law was always putting a phone in his hand and saying, 'It's your sister's birthday, call up and do something.' She made our relationship close. She could have pushed it apart, but she really worked at keeping it close.

Nevertheless, all the effort to build closeness may be fruitless if the effort is not responded to. Satisfying relationships are a two-way street, where each side needs to be responsive and appreciative of the other.

Among the many advantages of a good sibling-in-law relationship is the emotional and financial support it can offer. This emotional support is very important, especially when a parent dies, as this woman foresaw: 'Let's face it, my parents will not be around the rest of my life. For this reason, my sister and brother-in-law are very important to me.'

Siblings may also offer financial help in time of need. One woman said that she was forever grateful to her sister-in-law who, she later found out, had taken out a bank loan to lend her the money to buy a piano.

The following are other examples of the support that siblings-in-law can offer each other:

> For a year, we had my kid sister and her baby living with us when my brother-in-law was in Viet Nam. After they left, my husband took our four kids out for dinner, to thank them for being so nice to my sister and the baby. 'The big lesson to be learned,' he said, 'is that blood is thicker than water. When you are family, you must always be able to count on each other.'

> After my husband died, his brother and sister-in-law moved into this neighborhood to be with me and my children. My sister-in-law wanted to live next door so her husband could be a father to her children and mine.

> I moved to Chicago because my sister-in-law called and said, 'I'd like you to come out.' My six-year-old son and I lived with them for about three months. She was unbelievable in terms of support and kindness and generosity.

My husband is a workaholic. I felt very protected by my brother-in-law who lives three blocks away. When the kids had to be chauffeured or anything had to be done, my brother-in-law was always available. Now my son has a great deal of love for this uncle because he was over every single day while he was a little kid.

In contrast, however, siblings-in-law can also cause trouble. This man blamed the breakup of his marriage on his brother-in-law:

My brother-in-law was a no-good, worthless human being — rotten, subhuman. He was the cause of my divorce because if my wife had recognized him for what he was when we were married, we would still be married. But she couldn't. I was good to him to make her happy. He lived with me when he ran away from jail. I gave him, his girl, her three dogs and two kids a place to live. I gave him work and money, but he cheated me at every turn. He broke into my house, threatened me at knife-point to give him money for booze and drugs.

If people got along well with their own brothers and sisters, chances are they will get along with their siblings-in-law. One woman said:

I love my sister. We're very close, so it was easier to take her husband in my heart and love him.

However, if the sibling rivalry was never worked out, early childhood competitive feelings can be repeated in the sibling-in-law relationship. One woman said:

My husband's older brother — there's only 11 months between them — is the only brother he has. We live not even three miles apart, but I have never had a cup of coffee in his house. When we built our house, his wife said, 'Well, we're building a bigger one!' It's so silly, the competition. That's what it narrows down to, competition and rivalry.

In some sibling-in-law relationships, there is minimal contact because the people involved do not have the same interests, as this man said:

> We buy insurance from my brother-in-law, but whether we have a relationship or not I really don't know. I just see my wife and me as sort of different from them, living in different places, leading a very different life. Not everybody is like you, and they have reasons for doing things their way.

Strained relationships between parents-in-law and children-in-law are often tolerated because the parents and children want to maintain contact with each other. But siblings-in-law do not show as much tolerance — they may simply stop visiting or phoning. Similarly, although respect for an elder may prevent a person from being candid with his parents-in-law, he may not be as hesitant to speak his mind to his siblings-in-law, who are usually closer in age. One man said:

> I have no inhibitions to tell my sister-in-law to shove it when she gets on my nerves. You don't feel free to express negative feelings to mothers- and fathers-in-law as you do to your own generation.

Because of the ages of the people involved, sibling-in-law relationships generally last longer than relationships between parents-in-law and children-in-law, and they can be a valuable source of mutual friendship and help if all parties put forth the required effort.

SUGGESTIONS

All the parties have to want to make the relationship close. If one wants and the other doesn't, it won't work. What's more, sibling-in-law misunderstandings generally do not heal by themselves. They can, however, be repaired, but only if all siblings involved make a strong effort to talk with each other and share their gripes and viewpoints.

If you are the sibling who is getting married, be aware of the feelings of your brothers and sisters who have been close to you.

If you are the sibling who is feeling "left behind," you may not understand why you feel sad or disappointed. You may be dealing with a loss of companionship. You may also not understand the needs of the bride and groom to be alone. But it is crucial to understand that the recently married siblings have entered a new stage of their lives and are very involved with each other.

Pay attention to what may be keeping you from communicating with your siblings-in-law. You may have been taught to overlook slights, even though you are angry. Or you may be afraid that you will not be listened to anyway. Thoughts of "What's the use?" may discourage you. No one can read your mind. If you can't figure out the problem on your own and find you cannot discuss it with your in-law or spouse, talk to an understanding friend, relative, or therapist. It is important to share the problem with someone.

Try to understand what is going on inside yourself, then the other person. The new in-law also is undergoing changes and tensions. He does not yet know you or your ways of relating. He may, for example, perceive your attempts to become close with him as smothering, just as he may interpret your attempts to respect his privacy as withdrawal. For example, if you do not initiate phone calls, the sibling-in-law may think you lack interest in him or that you disapprove of him.

In the long run, efforts to communicate and keep in touch will make for a stronger relationship between you and your siblings and siblings-in-law that will enable you to enjoy each other's company.

Try to spend time with your siblings-in-law to get to know them. If it is difficult to have a physically close relationship with them because of geographic considerations, phoning and writing become important links.

*In foreign relations, as in all other relations,
a policy has been formed only when commitments
and power have been brought into balance.*

**WALTER LIPPMAN,
U.S. Foreign Policy, 1943**

VII

Balancing Loyalties

◆ *Everyone Wants to "Go Back Home Again"*
◆ *Whose Family Will we Visit for the Holidays?*
◆ *Some Parents Unfairly Pressure Their Grown Children to Visit*

Holidays and special occasions are times when families get together to celebrate, rekindle relationships and refuel the feelings of familial love. Married children often feel torn about which family to visit and are put into a position of keeping a "scorecard" to see whose turn is next.

Parents, parents-in-law, sisters- and brothers-in-law, and children may often tug and pull with demands, for example, to visit during the holidays or with requests to baby-sit, or ask for loans.

It is natural for parents to want to have their children present on special occasions, but this can put an unreasonable strain on the young married couple.

One social worker described such demands in the early years of her marriage:

It was assumed by all of us — the parents and us and everybody — that we would divide holidays and special occasions between them. There was never any thought that we would have any of it by ourselves, or with anybody else.

Often, both sets of parents demand equal time with the young couple, or the couple feel that they should spend the same amount of time with each set of parents. The social worker quoted above said that she and her husband felt that if they spent a certain number of hours with one set of parents, they had to spend an equal number of hours with the other set. Her mother-in-law had had the same problem in her marriage:

> My mother-in-law remembered the agony of her early marriage, and how exhausted she was on New Year's Day. She would have to be at three different places and have to drive 45 minutes between each place. So this goes back for generations.

Another woman said:

> My mother hated that her family got short shrift when she always spent holidays with her husband's family. She still has that kind of feeling with me — that I am giving her short shrift when I go to my in-laws.

Another woman described the psychological and emotional pain such demands caused her:

> My parents lived in New York. We live in New Jersey, near my in-laws, and if we spent one weekend with my parents in New York, we had to sleep at my in-laws' on Friday night even though they only lived six blocks away. We had to equalize down to the hour. On Thanksgiving we'd have two Thanksgiving dinners. It was like a tug of war and we were the rope.

Marriage does not imply that you must shed old loyalties, rather you will have to adopt new ones. A most important ingredient for a happy marriage is the loyalty to one's spouse. A frequent source of marital stress is a conflict between two sets of loyalties.

A psychologist, married four months, described his situation:

> I don't feel as compelled to visit my parents as much as my wife wants to go to hers. She doesn't really like going to my parents.

She feels more pulled by the shoulds and shouldn'ts of her family. Her aunts expect us to go to their kids' birthday parties. This is a little ridiculous. These kids are one and two years old.

One young woman said that when she was first married, she was torn between her husband and her family as to who came first:

When I got back from my honeymoon, the first thing I did was call my parents. It bothered me why I did it. I was never sure, should I call them the minute I walked into the house from work? I was confused. One day I decided that if my husband was not first, there would be a divorce. It wasn't something he had to point out to me.

One woman whose parents refused to attend her wedding, and whose husband has refused to talk to them for the past six years, was torn between feelings for her family and loyalty to her husband:

Every holiday — Mother's Day, Father's Day, birthdays — we always go to my husband's mother. Although she always tries to make it a very pleasant day, it just makes me feel the absence of my own parents even more. We're never sharing anything with them. They never have the pleasure of seeing us as a family, and there are times that my in-laws tell me I spoil many of their holidays because I am never happy being with them. It's not that I am not happy being with them, but I would be much happier if my parents could be there. To this day, if my parents come, my husband leaves the house.

Some parents exert a pull on their children that at times may be unreasonable and intrusive — or at least be seen as such by the young couple. One salesman told this about his father-in-law:

Every time we left town, he would demand that we call him every night. I'd say, 'Look, if something happens, you'll read about it in the newspapers first,' and I would not call him. The first few trips we took, my wife would sneak off and give him a call, but it got to the point where calling her parents to check in reset all the tensions and she started to say that it was better not to call them and just stay out of contact. Her father would call up and say, 'When are we going to see you?' If he heard we were with my parents, he accused us of spending more time with my parents than with him; whereas my parents, while they enjoy being with us, couldn't care less whether or not we are together every week.

One woman married ten years complained about her mother-in-law's demands:

During the first eight years of my marriage, my in-laws were living here in the city. I felt resentment whenwe had to go there every Sunday. It was even before we had children. I thought we should be able to do things ourselves. They were not active in any organization, so they really had nothing except us. My mother-in-law would call me every evening. I wasn't used to that. I was away from home a long time and was used to being independent.

People react to such demands in a number of ways. One woman, whose mother tried to arouse guilt in her by saying, "Well, you spent eight hours there and only five hours here," described her feelings:

My reaction was to say, 'Let's skip the whole thing.' I was frustrated. It all seemed impossible. But I was not the rebellious kind to say, 'If you don't like it, lump it,' and walk off. Instead I always tried to placate her and explain why it was that way.

Some people do not let themselves be pushed around. One woman said:

My husband and I were accustomed to spending our anniversary alone, but my mother-in-law wanted us to go to a party at someone's house. She wanted to make some kind of family deal on that weekend. I said no, we would not be available. And she said, 'Talk to him, he will go.' I said, 'It is our anniversary. He is not going to go, Mom. You know we always spend it together here alone.' 'Oh, so you will celebrate it another time,' she said. I said, 'No, I want to celebrate it this weekend,' and she said, 'I will talk to him.' I finally said, 'Listen, Mom, you know he will listen to me and not you.' She was silent, and had no expression on her face.

Parents often do not realize the problems their married children experience in trying to balance loyalties to their parents as well as to themselves.

Perhaps it is best for the parents to learn to understand and respect the young couple's need for privacy and time to solidify their relationship, as this mother of two divorced children eventually realized:

> Young people have enough to do to learn to live with each other. We should see them when they want to see us and just let them alone. And when they are ready, they will come to us.

These problems may be resolved as the parents become wiser and less demanding and the young couple become more assertive concerning their own needs and comforts.

SUGGESTIONS FOR PARENTS

Remember that your children cannot be in two places at the same time. Don't put unreasonable pressure on your children to spend time with you. Respect the couple's decision if they choose not to accept your invitation to visit.

SUGGESTIONS FOR CHILDREN

If you cannot or do not want to accept your parents' invitations, do not be evasive, tell them as soon as possible. Each spouse should respectfully answer any invitation or request by saying, "I must first check out our plans with my husband/wife." Hopefully, your parents will understand and respect your decision.

SUGGESTIONS FOR PARENTS AND CHILDREN

To get along better, it is wise to discuss this and all other areas of potential conflict. Especially the first year of marriage — parents, parents-in-law, sisters- and brothers-in-law and children — ought not to tug and pull with demands for visits and phone calls.

That which a person gives to another is never lost.

RABBI ELIJAHU DESSLER,
19th-century scholar,
author of "Strive for Truth"

VIII

Gifts And Financial Aid

- *People Give Gifts for Many Reasons*
- *Three Parts to Gift Giving — Learn Them*
- *Simple Politeness and Graciousness are Equal to Wind and Water in Changing Matters*

Gift giving is a gesture fraught with complicated feelings. Gift giving is more than a simple transfer of an object from one individual to another. The feelings and underlying reasons of the person who gives and the expectations of the person who receives play important roles in this seemingly simple act.

People give gifts for many reasons — to show that they care, to make a good impression, to atone for guilt, to bribe, or out of a sense of obligation. Some people give willingly and graciously, others begrudgingly, and still others with strings attached. The giver must think about how much he wants to spend, how much he can afford, what would be an appropriate gift, what the recipient might expect, whether the recipient would like the gift, or whether the recipient's family or peers will approve of his choice.

The recipient also has concerns at gift-giving time. Will he like the gift? Will the gift be useful? Does he really need this item? What will his family and friends think about the gift? How will the acceptance of this gift obligate him? These thoughts are most certainly prevalent, not only at major one-time events, such as weddings, but at annual occasions such as birthdays and anniversaries.

A gift is usually considered something freely given from one person to another for his benefit and pleasure. Parental gifts to newlyweds are not only gestures of good wishes and love but also helpful, practical items for a young couple starting to build a new life together. As time goes on, parental gift-giving may be expanded to also include services, such as baby-sitting, preparing dinners, being available in emergencies, and giving financial aid.

The respondents in this study described a wide range of feelings regarding gifts and financial aid, running the spectrum from appreciation to resentment. One man said:

> It was nice to receive. I still have the tallit (prayer shawl) my father-in-law gave me thirty years ago.

Most parents continue to give gifts to their married children long after the wedding is over. This mother-in-law of three married children expressed a prevalent attitude:

> I couldn't have a comfortable home, living with nice things, knowing that the children do not have the things they need. I believe in sharing and giving. If this one needed a refrigerator, I bought a refrigerator. If this one needs a bathroom set and I find I can afford it, I will buy it. They pick out whatever they like.

However, some parents expressed resentment about feeling obligated to continue giving to their married child. Having looked forward to freedom from the responsibility of parenthood, this woman was surprised to find that her son's marriage did not mean an end to her financial responsibility for him:

> We had been in the house for only four hours after our son's wedding and we had this wonderful feeling of relief — our son was off on his own. Then we got a phone call from an operator saying, 'Your son wants to make a long distance call and charge it to your number. Is it all right?' First of all, you say, 'Is he in some kind of emergency?' Then you think, 'Why can't he pay for

his own call?' Well, he would not ask if he could, so you say, 'Okay.' But that wonderful euphoria of 'Now he is on his own,' is completely gone.

Some people recognize that there are limits to the gifts and financial aid. This mother of eight said this about her older children:

Once they graduated from college, they were on their own. Nobody comes back to us for help, not that they couldn't, but they have not because they realize there are others behind them who really need it.

A widow living on a limited income told her married children:

That's it, kids. I am getting ready to retire. No more money. I will help you out with baby-sitting if I am not busy.

Though some parents are openly resentful, they continue to give gifts and financial aid to their children, as did this woman:

I give, and I am also resentful. When I give to my married children, I don't expect anything back, but I am not always happy with giving. It is a necessity. I want them to have what I think they should have.

Many middle-aged people describe feeling emotionally or financially burdened by having to care for parents, parents-in-law, unmarried children, newlywed children, divorced children, and grandchildren. Raised during the depression, these people live carefully, fearful of inflation. They do not see any repayment forthcoming from either their parents or their children. A 60-year-old woman said:

When my mother-in-law needed me, I went every day. By the end of the day, I was physically exhausted. I helped my mother, too. I was there twice last week. But I don't know if I will get that kind of attention from my kids when I get old. I don't expect it. It's a different generation.

Many parents are generous but do not want to be taken advantage of. They would like something in return — to spend time with their children, to be appreciated.

This mother wanted a response from her children:

> I wonder if we are spoiling them by giving too much. I'm always sending gifts and not even getting a thank-you card. I want to see them, so I say to my husband, 'They can't afford to come, let's give them tickets.' My husband will say he's not for it. But I will say, 'I miss them, I want to see them, it's six months.' So he winds up sending them the tickets. But I often wonder if they would save up enough money to see us on their own.

The growing number of divorces has made some parents apprehensive about giving gifts of great financial or sentimental value. Some even insist that their child and his fiancÈ sign a prenuptial agreement to keep such items in the family in the event of a divorce. This woman hesitated to give her son and daughter-in-law family valuables:

> Jack has lots of friends and has stood up at a great many weddings, three of which ended in divorce. His wife likes antiques. We have some that belonged to Jack's grandmother. I'm still debating how much of the antiques I want to give them. If I do give them, I want to clearly state that these are family things which belong to Jack. That is a horrible thing to say, and I don't know if it can really be done. It might cause more problems. I might be better off not giving them.'

Anthropologist Marcel Mauss pointed out in his book, *The Gift*, that in primitive societies there are three parts to gift giving: giving, receiving, and repayment. Gifts are given and received with the understanding that repayment is necessary. In our modern society, there are no specific rules regarding repayment of gifts, and its importance is often overlooked. In the Japanese culture the obligation of repayment is spelled out in the concept of *giri*, which this Japanese-born American woman described as follows:

If you are given something, you must repay it or do better. The mother-in-law, for most daughters-in-law, is someone you must respect and must treat very nicely. Although you may not feel that way, you have to act that way in order to please your own husband and family.

This man told about his Japanese-born wife:

When someone does something nice for you, you reciprocate, you don't forget. My wife thinks she has an obligation to cook something nice and take it over to my mother when she has some special fish my mother likes.

Repayment can be as simple as saying thank you, as this woman said:

If someone is nice enough to think of them, at least they can show a little thought and write thank-you notes. It doesn't cost anything.

Another stated:

Parents do expect something in return. It is a pile of curd that parents should always be on the giving end. Parents are complicated human beings. You are happy for your married children, but quietly in the back of your mind you wonder if they would ever pick up a pretty handkerchief for you. Parents like being surprised. I don't think they ever outgrow having needs, too, just like the children.

Many people in this study reported that gifts did flow in both directions. Children-in-law not only received gifts, but also gave gifts to their parents-in-law. Often, these gifts were non-material ones — gifts of the self, such as interest and affection. An 80-year-old woman told about her two sons-in-law:

They are very generous, not with money — I don't need that — but with concern. I am alone, up in years. My son-in-law who lives in town calls three or four times a week to say, 'How are you?' My other son-in-law travels a lot, but whenever he goes out of town, he will call me from wherever he is.

Accepting gifts is another aspect of gift exchange. Some who received gifts knew how to appreciate them for what they were. One woman said:

> His parents are in a position to help us financially, more so than my parents. We were married young, and they did above-and-beyond and still do to this day, tremendously. My parents probably supplied more emotional help. They can do that, so they do. Maybe strings are attached on all sides, but they are entitled to it. I don't see anything wrong with that.

Those who graciously accepted gifts reflected a positive attitude for their in-laws. One woman who loves her mother-in-law said:

> I never want to take back what she gives me. Even if there might be a better or sharper housecoat, I just want something she has given me. I stick the gloves she bought me in my pocket for her to see that I wear them.

Gift giving, however, does not always evoke positive feelings in the recipient. Some recipients were resentful because the gifts were either inadequate or given in place of a human connection. One young woman said:

> It's nice when your in-laws begin to know what you like and don't like. I once got a watch from my mother-in-law that had nothing to do with her taste or mine. I would rather not get a gift than get a gift so alien to my taste.

Another woman, with a new infant, said:

> I had to accept that my in-laws show their love by giving things like clothing and money to buy the comforts and little luxuries of life. I was brought up in a warm, loving home where physical gifts

were not stressed. For this reason, I will not be as close to my mother-in-law as I would like to be. She is very busy in the family business, with social obligations, as well as with beautician, manicure, pedicure, and shopping. Her time is rarely spent with her only grandchild in this city. This bothers me. She has never baby-sat for my son, something I consider more precious than gifts.

A third woman felt owned by accepting financial aid from her mother-in-law:

She invested $10,000 in each of her kids' names and told them years ago that this would be used for a house down payment. She expects to be repaid for it by 'owning' us. If we tried to repay her, she would be insulted. She likes to hold it over our heads periodically. I am sorry that we could not afford the house without their help. But in their own way, my in-laws enjoy supporting their kids. It makes them feel needed, I guess.

A parent's help may be acceptable to his child but unacceptable to his child-in-law. One woman said:

Jim's family life is completely different from mine. My mom waits on you hand and foot, and Jim's mother is not like that. My mom thinks he doesn't like her because he won't let her do for him.

Both men and women described their discomfort in accepting gifts. Some needed to assert their own independence, others refused to be intruded upon or allow their affection to be bought with gifts. This woman explained why she refused to accept gifts from her parents-in-law:

Part of the problem was that we were living in their home. We had to assert our independence from them by saying 'no' when my mother-in-law said we had to have a color TV set or a movie camera.

One father of six felt that his ability was being criticized:

> When my side of the family gives us presents, I feel they want to help us out. But when my wife's father gives it, it indicates we are not self-sufficient. It's not like a present, it's semi-charity. I think if I was financially secure, I would not look at it as such.

This man was convinced that his in-laws tried to buy his affection:

> I see my in-laws as trying to buy their way into hearts with gifts instead of with their personalities, because their personalities are so abrupt, though deep down their intentions are honorable. They see money and gift giving as being the way to bridge the gap with people. It bothered me to see that they always gave a gift with a price tag on it.

Some were disappointed because they received few gifts and little financial help from their parents-in-law. One person cynically said, "The gift we received was a grave plot, which we gave to an aunt who wanted it and now uses it." Another man told about his mother-in-law, who humiliated him when he asked for help:

> I figured I would borrow a couple of hundred from my mother-in-law. The insurance was due, rent was due, hospitalization was due, and my wife was pregnant with the first one. She had ten grand on hand from an insurance settlement but said, 'No, get a loan. I don't have any money.' I said, 'Don't do it for me, do it for your daughter and your unborn grandchild.' What was so bad was that that was the Thursday I got laid off. Now, on Thursday night she said she didn't have the money and on Saturday she went out and bought an $800 TV set and paid cash for it. I never said a word to her again.

Another source of disappointment is gifts that are promised but never given. This woman expressed her disappointment with her mother-in-law:

Before the wedding, she said she was going to make me a gown, and before we had a baby she said she was going to get me a rocking chair. And before we moved, she said she was going to get me a stove. None of these things ever came to be. She means well, but she should not offer.

As a person matures, his attitude about gifts may change. A woman married twice said she now feels differently about receiving gifts from her parents-in-law:

The second time around, you accept anything because of maturity and experience. You do anything not to cause trouble, and it has marvelous dividends. For seven years in a row, my mother-in-law gave me for my birthday dusting powder which she picked up in a church bazaar. I don't even use dusting powder, but I say, 'Thank you. That is just what I wanted.'

Some people do not know how to give gifts graciously, others do not show others do not know how to accept them, and still others do not know how to repay them.

Children learn to give and to receive by example. One of the important functions of a parent is to give freely and appropriately to his child, and this is how children learn to give as they grow. Parents must also teach children how to receive graciously, which is an art in itself. It takes practice, experience, and good will to give and receive and repay in an appropriate manner.

SUGGESTIONS

"Simple politeness and graciousness are equal to wind and water in changing matters." (unknown author). Do not underestimate the importance of saying "Please, thank you, excuse me," at the appropriate times.

Whether it is better to give than to receive depends in great part on the circumstances. In either case, one must learn some of the basic rules:

Give items that you think the recipient would like, might need, or find useful. In order to determine what those items may be, you could ask the recipient or someone who is close to that person and knows his likes and dislikes. Bridal registries at department stores can be most helpful for newlyweds.

Don't give gifts which may be an unnecessary burden or clutter. If you cannot afford to give gifts of great financial value, you can nevertheless express your good wishes in words or actions. A gift need not always be a material one.

If you are the recipient of a gift, you must not overlook the important aspect of repaying the gift by saying thank-you with a phone call, a visit, or a very special note.

*Therefore shall a man leave his father and his
mother and shall cleave unto his wife.*

Genesis II, 25

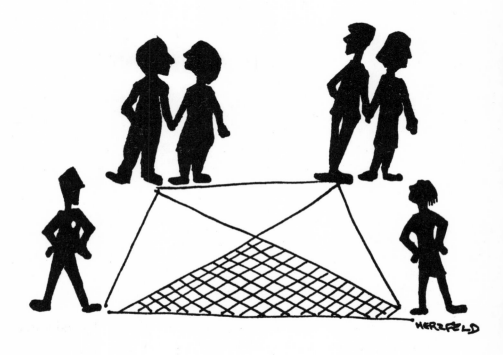

IX

The In-Law Triangle

♦ *Emotional Ties Between Parent and Child Endure Forever*
♦ *Seven Variations of Triangles Describe the Parent/Adult Child/and In-Law Relationship*
♦ *The Parental Law of Inertia*

Being a parent-in-law involves new rules. Parents no longer have the same privileges they had before their child's wedding. First-time parents-in-law may find guidance in folk-sayings which place the onus on them: "Keep your mouth shut and wear beige." "Keep your pocketbook open and your lips closed." A German proverb says, "Remember the three S's: "Schenken, schveigen, and schlungen." Freely translated it means: "Be generous with gifts; be quiet and refrain from giving advice; swallow the insults and hurts that you may receive." A Yiddish maxim says, "Az tsvei leigen oif ain Kishen, darf der driter nit mishen. "When two people lie on one pillow, a third person must not mix in." These directives, which may sound harsh, are reminders to the older and, hopefully, wiser parent-in-law to display self-control.

When a person marries and leaves his family in order to start a new one, he may be concerned that the ties to his old family will be severed. Be assured that the emotional ties between parent and child endure a lifetime. These ties may be stretched, but they are never broken. These old and new ties form what can be called the "in-law triangle," and are, in reality, two overlapping triangles.

His Parents   Her Parents

Husband   Wife

Our society stresses the importance of independence and "making it on your own." Newlyweds, influenced by these ideas, may at first try to cut these ties and deny any needs they may have for their parents. Indeed, the young couple must pull away from their parents initially — they need time and privacy to get to know each other and establish themselves as a separate new unit — and the parents might also pull away initially to give the young couple this opportunity.

Immediately following the wedding, some parents experience a sense of depletion, which they describe as "feeling empty and depressed." This feeling is normal and quite common. Although the parents are happy to be relieved of the responsibilities for the child who has just married, they do not want to lose their child's affection. This mother expressed her initial fears that she had lost her son:

> I cried like a baby when Tim got married. I thought I lost him because he had another Number One. My daughter said, 'You're crazy, Mom, he'll be back.'

In fact, as a psychoanalyst Anna Orenstein has pointed out, a continued relationship with the grown child is very important to a parent's self-esteem and well-being. Some parents may not understand the newlywed child's need to distance himself from his parents and may make unreasonable demands on the child. A psychologist told his mother:

> Please don't make me choose between you and my wife. I love you both, but in different ways. If it's a matter of choosing, you will lose.

After the initial distancing from their parents, the newlyweds may become more sure of themselves, and they are more willing to acknowledge these ties. The parties in each triangle — parent, child, and child-in-law — may then begin to interact with each other in more mature ways.

Much research has been done about the parent/infant relationship; less about the parent/grown-child relationship; and almost nothing about the parent/adult child/child-in-law relationship. A very important part of this in-law triangle is the relationship between the parent and the adult child, the tone of which will affect the relationship with the child-in-law.

In this study, seven types of parent/adult child/child-in-law interactions emerged. In the first type, the spouse acts as a spokesman for the married child in dealing with the adult child's parents. Some spouses express the married child's love for the parents by writing, calling, and making plans to get together with the in-laws. They serve as the link which keeps the parent and the child connected. Others express the married child's anger toward his parents, as did these three people:

Perhaps it gives my husband satisfaction to hear me vent against his parents. It enables him to vent his anger against them through me.

There is something in the mother/daughter relationship that says a mother can't be wrong. No matter how right the daughter is, she always feels like she is going up against something in the Super Bowl when she tackles her mother. Her mother always know where to hit. My wife's way of retaliation was claming shut and walking away. I come from a family where we let loose, and many times I took her family on, one on one.

My mother called this morning about two or three minutes after seven. My husband knows how it irritates me when she calls so early. He gets on the phone and very gently says, "Ma, was it so important to get your daughter out of bed with this?' From him, she took it just fine because when I got on the phone, she said, 'I'm really sorry. Your husband is absolutely right.' If I would have said it, she would have hung up crying.

The married child may be aware and appreciate that his spouse functions as a spokesman for him. Others may not be aware and may therefore feel caught up in the middle of arguments between parents and spouse. Using a spouse to express anger may also backfire, as this woman pointed out:

> I complained about my mother to my husband. At the time, I needed a champion when my mother did not understand me. Now, nine years later, my mother understands me, but my husband hasn't changed. He's still angry at her, and I'm not.

In the second type of interaction, the married child uses the spouse as a means of distancing himself from his parents, as the following people explained:

> One of the bonuses of getting married is having a husband who is your best excuse. You can always blame him if you don't want to do something.

> I do not want to give up my special relationship with my parents. I want all the goodies and gifts that my status as the 'baby' brings. Instead, I use my husband as a scapegoat. He is the excuse I use not to move back near my parents.

In the third type of interaction, the married child talks to his parents directly. The spouse does not act as spokesman for him. This woman avoided confrontations with her parents-in-law:

> I decided, when it comes to conflicts, to let my husband take care of his parents. I never talk to them about problems. There's pleasantness, not bitterness, with me. In the long run, they will forgive him and accept whatever he says, whereas with me they'd always remember the disagreements.

In the fourth type of interaction, the married child again does not assert himself to a parent, but the spouse does not speak up for him, as in this man's case:

My wife abdicates and regresses in front of her parents. We talked
about it. I gave her an ultimatum: she must speak up to her
parents, otherwise I won't go see them anymore. She has to play
a more active role, or else I won't go to my in-laws.

In a variation of this, the married child does not assert himself to
his parents, but instead expresses his anger to his spouse, as this
woman noted:

My husband would never face up to his mother to say, 'Don't say
that about my wife.' He had the lack of tact to come and tell me
what she said. One way of getting pressure off is telling me, and
then I get mad. I told him time and time again. 'Don't tell me
these things. I'm better off if I don't know.'

In the fifth type of interaction, some parents behave according to
what I call the "parental law of inertia." This means that they
continue to treat their married children as though they were still
little. A 32-year-old married career woman whose mother still
reminds her to use the bathroom before she leaves the house said, "I
wonder if parents ever see their child as having fully grown up and
being totally functional."

A married child may be guilty of inertia, too. He may continue to
allow things "to drift" and wait for someone else to improve an
unpleasant situation. He may behave like a small child in the
presence of his parents or when discussing matters concerning his
parents. He may be inhibited from discussing in-law problems with
his spouse or parents-in-law. One woman said, "It took me 30 years
to ask my husband why he didn't like my mother." Another said:

If I had been wiser, I would have said, 'This is terrible. We have
to do something about this in-law situation. Let's talk with my
parents.' My husband was just not very nice to them, and it got
worse and worse.

In the sixth type of interaction, parents act toward their children
in an arbitrary and unreasonable manner. One father demanded
immediate repayment from his newlywed son for all the college

tuition he had paid. The couple felt victimized, controlled, and manipulated, unable to experience a sense of autonomy. They protected themselves by avoiding the parent. Such inappropriate parental behavior demeans and angers the adult child and child-in-law.

Another example of unreasonable behavior is parents who insist the young couple "make it on your own" without giving them financial help. But "making it on your own" contradicts reality. There is always someone who helps us, if not with money, at least with words of encouragement, or knowledge. Many of the parents in this study did give emotional and financial support to married children. But such support is not always accepted, as this woman said:

> My husband shunned my parents' offers to help. We never did accept anything financially or emotionally. A rift occurred, and everyone suffered because of it.

In the seventh type of interaction, the parents blame the child-in-law for any difficulties between the child and child-in-law or between the parents and their child, as this man pointed out:

> My parents loved to have us over the traditional Friday night dinner and Sunday visit every week, but I didn't want to spend that much time on that frequent of a basis. Of course, my parents always blamed my wife because we didn't come.

Regardless of the type of interaction, there may be some degree of jealousy in almost all in-law triangles. Nearly every bride feels sensitive and competitive about the loyalty her husband feels for his family. As one bride put it, "At first, I think I was jealous when my husband would do things for his family." A groom also may feel sensitive and jealous of the affection his wife continues to feel for her parents, as this woman pointed out: "When my mother calls and my husband answers the phone, he'd say to me, 'Your other husband is on the phone.'"

Irritations may soar when couples discuss each other's parents or siblings, primarily because criticism of one's family is often interpreted as criticism of one's self. One woman said, "When he criticizes my mother, I feel he criticizes me." One newlywed said, "When my wife tells me what she dislikes about my family, my hackles rise." A woman said, "When I'm angry, I'll pick on his folks and say, 'You're a liar like your Dad,' or 'a thief just like your brother.'" Another man said, "At times, it is impossible to discuss our folks."

Some couples completely avoid discussing parents, at least initially. One woman said, "I don't want him to think I am bad-mouthing his parents." Another said:

> I don't think I ever said anything about his family for the first few years because I wanted to please him. But I found that after a while it wasn't pleasing him any more than it was pleasing me. Then I began to voice an opinion as to how I felt about his mom.

After a while, feelings of being criticized may diminish. A woman married 12 years said:

> We used to have a lot of conflict in conversations about parents. Now it's gotten better. I hope we never get back into that kind of comparison of families.

The husband's and wife's sensitive and jealous feelings will decrease as they receive the reassurance that is the outgrowth of love and acceptance. Reciprocated love between the husband and wife and mutual acceptance between the couple and the parents-in-law will lead to a reduction in the feelings of jealousy. The converse is also true. Without the love and acceptance, the rift and the anger will continue to grow.

Parents may also initially feel jealous at the thought of losing their child's affection to another person and family. This parental jealousy decreases if the child and child-in-law express interest in the parent, as this woman said:

> You want to know you're important, to know you're respected, to know that what you do is appreciated and means something. You don't want to be taken for granted.

The interest, however, should be reciprocated by the parent, as this woman did:

> My mother-in-law was never interested in who I was or what I did. I was determined to be different. I made a point of showing interest in my future daughter-in-law.

The goal for each person in the parent/adult child/child-in-law triangle is to continue to develop as an individual while maintaining caring, supportive ties with the others.

As adult children continue to mature, parents may come to accept the fact that their relationship with them has changed. Parents may also continue to mature after their children marry, and their focus may shift from their children and children-in-law's careers to a broader range of interests. Thus, the tie between a parent and child need never be broken, only expanded to include the child's spouse.

SUGGESTIONS TO PARENTS OF THE MARRIED CHILD

Unless you get along better with your child-in-law than with your own child, it is generally better to talk directly with your child, rather than your child-in-law, about sensitive subjects such as finances, holiday plans, visits, naming a child, religion, etc. Usually, no matter what you may say to your child about these areas of possible disagreement, he is more likely to forgive and forget than a child-in-law, who, especially early into he marriage, may not yet understand your family's ways of handling problems.

Even when the disagreement is major — for example, if your child marries someone of another faith and you feel that your values and heritage have been rejected — keep your ties to your child intact by phoning and writing. Even though you may feel hurt and disappointed, your child is still very important to you, just as you are to him.

SUGGESTIONS TO THE MARRIED CHILD

Most parents and parents-in-law want to remain important in the lives of their married adult children. A bride made her mother-in-law very happy the day of the wedding when she said, "Thank-you very much for your son." That's exactly what the mother-in-law wanted to hear, that her son, her contribution to the marriage, was appreciated. And the comment implied that the mother, too, was a valued asset.

Be courteous and gracious to your parents-in-law. The payoff is immeasurable.

Some in-laws don't get hurt easily, others do. Unless you get along better with your parents-in-law than with your own parents, it is probably wiser to negotiate with your own parents about sensitive issues, especially early in the marriage. Later, as you come to know your parents-in-law better and become more at ease with them, you may be able to discuss issues of possible disagreements directly with them.

No matter what your age, you usually remain precious to your parents. Therefore, when there is a disagreement between you and your parents, it is generally better for you, the adult child, rather than your spouse, the son-in-law, to discuss the controversial issue with your own parents. The disagreement thus becomes a "family discussion" without excessive strain. Touchy matters such as financial requests, vacation plans, holiday visits, baby's names, etc., can often be more easily resolved in this manner. You have had about twenty or more years' experience living with your parents, and you know their quirks and foibles inside and out. Your anger and annoyance are more likely to be forgiven and forgotten by your parents than by your parents-in-law. Most parents forgive their children more readily than their children-in-law.

The important thing is not to sever connections with your parents or parents-in-law over misunderstandings and disagreements. Misunderstandings can be cleared up, and disagreements can be clarified. Parents are an important part of your life. Don't cut yourself off from them.

All real living is meeting — when we are persons to one another we are not objects to be experienced nor an "it" to be used . . . but an I and a Thou standing in mutuality of recognition and relation.

MARTIN BUBER,
20th-century philosopher

CHAPTER

See Me
As I Am

- *In-Laws, too, Have Blind Spots*
- *Recognize the Multi-Facets of Your In-Law's Personality*
- *Temper Your In-Law Criticism*

A deeply moving complaint often expressed by children-in-law is: "My in-laws don't see me as I am." This complaint is unlike others in which parents-in-law are accused of being critical, possessive, jealous, demanding, hostile, or intrusive. The crux of this complaint is that either parents-in-law do not recognize the young person's total worth or they want that person to be different. "To my father-in-law," one woman said, "I was always just 'that girl from Chicago' that his son married." The individuality and talents of the child-in-law are not always fully appreciated. "I am a writer," one man said, "but my father-in-law wants me to be a commodities broker." Each of the following three complaints expresses similar dissatisfaction:

I am married eight years. My mother-in-law does not know who or what I am. I am a writer. She is still surprised that I can cook. She convinced herself from day one that I couldn't cook because I was a career woman.

My mother-in-law does not see me as I am. I'm constantly trying to assert myself in all kinds of silly ways to shake her out of her complacency in who I am and what I am — sometimes in ways I am ashamed of, saying things that are a little more radical than I actually feel to get a rise out of her. But she doesn't hear it, she never hears me.

My mother-in-law was shocked by the fact that I'm not a secretary. I used to be a secretary, but when I told her my salary and that I'm an editor, not a secretary, she asked my husband, 'Isn't she still just a secretary?' That indicates how she regards me.

There is a universal human need for recognition and confirmation — all of us need to be admired and appreciated for what we are.

Being overestimated is as uncomfortable as being underestimated, and equally frustrating is being treated as an object to be displayed. In the following two cases, the women complained because they were not being seen as they really were.

All my mother-in-law does is say, 'You're marvelous, you're terrific.' When I complained of having problems at work, her reaction was, 'It must be their fault. You're so perfect, how can they be doing this to you? There has to be something wrong with them.' It's not all their fault. I do have problems, and I would like to talk about them with her.

My mother-in-law always tells me how she is constantly bragging about me. Why she feels the need to tell me that, I don't know. I don't appreciate that because it's very shallow. My in-laws want me to be a reflection of themselves, so they're taking the good things without any genuine interest in me.

Much human difficulty results from not hearing, not seeing, not listening. If one listens and responds to another, he has the basic ingredients for an on-going, satisfying relationship, but it requires being responded to and understood in return. To see a person as he really is takes time and energy and willingness.

This woman was disappointed about her mother-in-law, who is close, yet so far away:

What I wanted was for somebody to really know who I was. I felt that my mother-in-law, a music critic, would be intellectually closer to me than my own mother. Here was a woman who could appreciate me and give me feedback on things that were really important. Instead, I found that my mother-in-law was somebody I do ritual things with, like having dinner with and buying Mother's Day presents for. But as far as really getting close, I can't and she can't.

This daughter-in-law also was frustrated by her parents-in-law:

They're nice, but we communicate on a different wavelength. If I didn't like them it would be simpler, but I do. And I think they genuinely care about me. My frustrations come because anything I do that's important to me short of having a child is really not a priority of theirs. They're not sensitive to what's important to me as an individual.

Parents who are unwilling to accept the child-in-law as he is and want him to do things their way are often viewed as critical and intrusive. As a result, the child-in-law does not feel respected for what he is or does, and dissatisfaction ensues. People feel drained and angered by constant criticism. Psychoanalyst Arnold Goldberg stated that an injury to one's self-esteem is worse than an injury to one's body. One woman said:

You can hurt somebody so many times with criticism that it's very difficult to repair the damage — like chipping a fine piece of crystal. You can grind it down, but you'll always know that it was chipped. My mother-in-law criticized me an awful lot about my weight, and the way I kept house.

This woman was infuriated by her Chinese sister-in-law's behaving like the stereotypical mother-in-law:

I think my sister-in-law would like to get me to change. Her 'friendly advice' is not done daily, but it's done regularly. It's the sort of thing like, 'You shouldn't use fitted sheets, you should use the others.' Well, I always use fitted sheets. I like fitted sheets. If

I'm having a good day, I can brush it off and not let it get to me. On the other hand, if I'm not having a good day, then I think I am going to kill her if she mentions it one more time.

As mentioned before, a basic human need is to have positive affirmation and acceptance. This can be a problem with people who are not yet sure of themselves. One woman, married at 18, said:

The problem with my marriage is that I don't know who I am yet. So how can I expect my in-laws to seeme as I am, if I'm not sure of who I am?

Another woman tried to do what she thought her mother-in-law would like:

I always felt that I had to sell myself to him. He was religious, and I would purposely say to him, 'I went to church!' I thought it would make him like me better. I was sort of being a people pleaser, a daughter-in-law like he wanted. I was a little dishonest because I wanted to be accepted, but I really did not know who I was myself.

The intense need for confirmation by others may diminish as one grows more confident and certain about himself. One man said:

I think I grew up and recognized that I had been insecure. I think it's what has happened inside of me that has changed my relationship with my in-laws.

This man felt little need for affirmation from in-laws:

I don't look for any appreciation from my in-laws. I don't feel any lack of appreciation in my life, so there's nothing that I'm looking for that I'm not receiving from them.

The "See Me As I Am" problem is not restricted to the younger generation. Very often, the adult child-in-law does not correctly perceive the parents. This could be related to the child-in-law's relative immaturity. When one is uncertain about oneself, one may also be unsure of who the in-laws are and how to respond to them. This woman explained her inability to see her in-laws clearly:

> What interferes with my seeing is that I spend an incredible amount of time tuning out. When you're worried about yourself, part of the survival technique is to tune out. Sometimes the obvious is right there, yet I miss my in-law's feelings.

Old needs from a person's childhood may interfere with seeing things as they really are. One woman whose parents had died when she was still a child realized only after years of psychotherapy that these losses were affecting her view of her mother-in-law:

> There were moments when my mother-in-law softened and I softened. But then I went back to resenting that she was alive and my mother was dead. It appeared at the time that I had no feeling for my mother-in-law, but it was my inability to have compassion or closeness for anyone. As I got older, I realized my input into the problems.

Another variation of the "See Me As I Am" problem occurs when people do see each other as they are, but do not like what they see. One woman reported how disturbed she was to see that her daughter-in-law had the same quick temper she had. Another woman was dissatisfied with her mother-in-law:

> I wish she weren't so insulated. I guess I'm trying to expose her to the world. Why is it so important? Maybe because I identify with her. I'm trying to improve her.

With time, some learn to accept the in-laws as they are, as this man did:

> In the beginning it was difficult to see her the way she was because I wanted her to be something more than she was. She didn't have any polish. She didn't come from a monied family. She didn't mix with high society. But she was a lovely woman, and in time

I came to appreciate that. She never put on airs, no pretenses, never interfered with anything, was always loving.

Only when people recognize and accept each other as individuals with unique characteristics and abilities can tensions between them diminish. This is as true of in-law relationships as it is of other human relationships.

SUGGESTIONS

If you have been offended or hurt by an "in-law" — it is easy to get angry, then pick out something you don't like about that person and remain critical of that person. You may begin to look for more things you don't like about him. The memory of the injury often remains unless the matter is discussed and cleared up. By remaining angry, focusing only on the negative, and ignoring his good points you are not seeing the complete person. As a result your long-term relationship with him may suffer.

For the sake of a better relationship with your in-law, take the time to try to get to know him — his good points, his accomplishments, his interests. Just as you can acquire an appreciation of music and of art, so, too, can you acquire an appreciation of an individual.

Trust your judgment, but don't be judgmental. Give your in-law the benefit of the doubt. You need not deny your feelings or ignore what you dislike about your in-law, but give him a chance to show his other facets. He is, after all, multidimensional, just as you are.

The parents have a new task to accomplish, to encompass the husband of their daughter or wife of their son in their own family, and in their own psychic system as an object of love.

THERESE BENEDEK,
psychoanalyst and author

CHAPTER
XI

Growth
And Change

- *The In-Law Relationship Grows and Changes*
- *Improved Relationships Come with Age, Wisdom, and Compassion*
- *Sadly, Some Relationships Stagnate and Even Deteriorate*

Although the in-law relationship officially begins at the marriage ceremony, the process of becoming an in-law begins as soon as the child announces his intention to marry.

The parents' reaction to this announcement varies, depending upon whether this is the first child in the family to be married (parents may react differently to the first child's announcement, compared to, say, the third child's announcement); how old the child is (parents may be more apprehensive about an 18-year-old's decision than a 28-year-old's); and whether the parents have previously known, and approved of, their child's fiancÈ or his family. It also depends on the maturity of the parent.

Some parents may be pleased by the news, but others — especially if the child is young and the first to be married — may feel dazed and say something like, "What's your hurry?" "Are you sure you know what you're doing?" "You're too young, wait a while." Such remarks may simply reflect the parents' own feelings about becoming parents-in-law. They do not necessarily imply rejection of their child's choice of mate.

Children usually want their parents' approval about their decision but may not realize that their parents can be thrown off balance by the sudden news. They may therefore be hurt and angered by their parents' remarks and may interpret them as disapproval or as attempts to control their lives. This may be the beginning of problems between the parents, adult children, and children-in-law.

Some parents turn to friends or relatives for advice on how to start off on a good footing with the prospective in-law, as did this woman:

> When my son told us, 'I'm engaged,' I did not know what to do first. I called my brother-in-law who had married off two children. He told us, 'First meet her parents, next buy the girl a present, and then send flowers.'

After resolving the initial problem of what to do first, people begin thinking about what to do to have a good long-term relationship with their new in-laws. Some parents are determined not to repeat what was done to them by their parents-in-law:

> When my daughter got married, I gave a lot of thought to the relationship I was going to have with her husband. I tried to remember all the things that bothered me about my in-laws. Things that bothered me, I tried not to do.

> I don't try to run their lives because I know when I was younger I didn't want anyone to run mine. In the early days, when my mother-in-law asked me to do something, I always resented it.

> I'll never call our kids on Sunday before noon because my mother-in-law calls us at 9:00 a.m., asking, 'Are you sleeping? How come you're sleeping?' I have nothing else to do on Sunday, why shouldn't I sleep?

Some try to compensate for past injuries, as did this woman:

> My in-laws demoralized me, destroyed my emotional fiber. I only know things not to do. I don't know any of the things I'm supposed to do. Now I think I'm being over nice to my daughter-in-law to compensate for my past.

Others decided that there are no rules to follow and that it takes common sense and time to build a relationship:

I don't think there are any rules. Just treat a mother-in-law or daughter-in-law like someone you would like to make your friend. You can be a better friend than a daughter or a mother. Then you will put your best foot forward and share something of yourself with them.

After a while, in-laws become like family. You get to know their ways, and what to expect.

When my son and his wife were first married, he had not lived in this area for three years. After he moved back to the city, there was no baseline of what to expect as to who visited whom, who called on whom, what we did on family holidays, vacations, who we informed in time of trouble. Because of the uncertainty, everyone had to feel his way along. Now we know what to expect.

Some people, both parents and married children, refrain from voicing any opinion that might cause problems with their in-laws:

I say and do nothing to interfere. I want to be on good terms and have the companionship with the grandchildren. I will not criticize the way my daughter-in-law raises the children. I don't know if my way is better.

It doesn't pay to fight with your in-laws over anything. It's not like a marriage where if there is a problem you have to work it out. I don't say things to my mother-in-law that I say to my mother. I'm careful not to say things that will never be forgiven.

My in-laws never saw their children as adults. You could never say to them what you wanted because they took it as disrespectful.

Others, however, are assertive in their relationship with their in-laws:

With her parents, it was mandatory to set them straight how things were going to be. Once I took that stand, everybody could function, but as long as I wanted to be a good boy, as long as I didn't stand on my own, it was a mess.

We were married ten years and in financial difficulty. When my father-in-law told me what to do, I grabbed him by the arm, took him out on the front porch, and said, 'See that address? That's my house. I runit the way I want.'

I never fought with my mother-in-law, but I told her straight out how I felt. She understood it, and that's when we started to have a better relationship. When she accused me of not taking care of my own children, I said, 'You know, you have a big mouth. How dare you say that?' We came to an understanding where she respected me. She liked the idea that I was straight with her.

Although many seek frank, open communication with their in-laws, it is difficult to obtain it:

I worked hard for a long time opening communications with my mother-in-law, but it's difficult for her to get into talking. She does not deal at that level. She will change the subject, she will deny. Then I get mad and withdraw.

If my mother-in-law would just really tell me what she felt and what she wanted, it wouldn't bother me. I could deal with her and say, 'I don't agree with you.' But she's so subtle and so indirect in her approach that I just get irritated.

After the in-law relationships have gone on for a while, they may make dramatic turnarounds for the better. These women described improvements in their in-law relationships:

Believe it or not, there's been a total reversal. Things are super. We've gotten to a point where my Mom is close to my husband and I'm close to his parents. His parents visit with me often, so they see things from my point of view.

The first visit, my father-in-law didn't want to come. He felt he would be in the way. He is the kind that would just sit and watch television. I rarely spoke to him. I had no relationship with him except to answer a question if he would address it to me. I never looked him in the face. I was very shy. Since they moved to New York three years ago, they come visit us for two weeks each year. On the whole, we have become closer because 'Absence makes the heart grow fonder.' I didn't mind them being in the house day and night, two weeks. I started talking more with my father-in-law, and he became more talkative.

My father-in-law thought I was after his son's money. He didn't trust me. That was the feeling I always got. Talking to him is awkward, but it becomes easier each time. I know what to say and what not to say, the questions to ask, the small talk to make. Steer clear of heavy issues, is what I've learned. And I think my father-in-law has warmed up to me a bit. He's more relaxed.

The improvement in the relationship is often the result of a deliberate effort by one or both of the parties involved, as the following examples show:

I had been married before and had a child. It was difficult for my mother-in-law to accept the fact that her son married a woman with a child. After years, I won her over. She came to love me very much. I did everything for her because I wanted my husband to be happy and wanted to be a family unit. I knew I had to accept her for her feelings toward me. Through the years she loved me because I earned it.

A human relationship is a thing that you develop. I took my mother-in-law in to live with us because I didn't like the way she was treated by the rest of the family. I'm a humanitarian, and I was willing to bend alot. But my wife and I proceeded along an uneven course because of that extra outside pressure of her mother coming to live with us.

In 13 years, my daughter-in-law and I never made it. Our relationship got worse and worse. I didn't care about my daughter-in-law, but I did care for my son. I said to him, 'Why don't we just turn the page and start from day one? Forget what happened.' I went there and had a lovely afternoon. I won't say she is going to change or that I am going to change, but at least we are talking, and I did do something about it.

At first, it was very strained. My husband and I lived on the first floor, and my son and daughter-in-law lived on the second. My grandson would come down to visit. My daughter-in-law wasn't too keen on that. She thought we were spoiling him, and she also thought she didn't have enough privacy. We decided we would just have to get along with her. We only have one son, and we don't want him taken away from us. She's a lot warmer toward us now than in the beginning.

Sometimes, the improvement comes about as a result of circumstances such as illness, birth of a child, financial gain or loss, moving, or aging. This woman told how her father-in-law changed as he aged:

My father-in-law ruled the family. My husband worked for him, and we lived nearby. We had no money. Everything we had, my father-in-law bought. Finally, I said I could not live near him any more, I could not see our marriage survive under those pressures. He had a violent temper. During one argument about our leaving the city, he chased me with a knife. He didn't want his son to leave. For many years after we left, I had a lot of hostility for this man. He wouldn't speak to us until a long time later. Now all is more or less forgiven, and he is just a sad old man.

However, not all relationships improve with time. This woman described how the relationship with her mother-in-law deteriorated as she became more assertive:

I said to her husband, 'We've got to do something about your mother,' and he said, 'She's a problem to you, you do something about it.' I did. I began to work on being very up-front. I put limits on her and said, 'You just cannot walk into our home, you have to at least knock on the door.' I was soon aware that my role in the family was as a servant. As long as I was a good servant, that was fine. The minute I didn't know my place, I certainly was not a good servant any more.

A few relationships show no change. One man said, "It started bad and ended bad, it had no possibility to go down and no incentive to go up." Most relationships, however, do change, for better or for worse.

Although relationships may change as the result of only one person's efforts, the chances for improvement are greater when there is an on-going effort by both parent-in-law and child-in-law, as these women described:

> Change doesn't just happen. There has to be a real interacting. I always try to work it out. It's a dynamic creative happening to solve problems. There has to be real giving and real receiving.

> My mother-in-law and I have developed a close relationship over the years because I don't think either one of us has ever wanted to hold grudges or to use a fight or a disagreement as an excuse to break off the relationship. I think I've learned over time that a willingness to have a close relationship is probably the mostimportant thing. Two people who are willing to compromise, to forgive, or to accept the weaknesses of the other can build a relationship.

Building a relationship with an in-law is not always an easy task. It requires a great deal of determination and effort on the part of both parties. The process takes time and demands a careful balancing of interest in the other person, with a respect for his privacy. It also requires the knowledge and understanding that each of you has needs which may differ, but that you will nevertheless accept.

SUGGESTIONS

Just knowing that most in-law relationships grow and improve over time may be instructive and reassuring. But remember that change for the better takes effort — be attentive and respectful. Value your in-laws as individuals.

The role of parent-in-law does not include some of the privileges of parenthood. Do not offer suggestions or phone your married children as freely as you did before they married. Step back, and refrain from unsolicited suggestions, especially during the first year of the couple's marriage. Be assured that when the couple need you they will call.

Since parents and children are bound up with invisible emotional ties, why not be bound up comfortably? If you feel uncomfortable with your in-laws, do something about it. If time, maturity, and wisdom don't help, chapters XVI and XVII may.

*East is east and west is west and
ne'er the twain shall meet.*

RUDYARD KIPLING

CHAPTER
XII

His Parents
And Hers

◆ *Three Categories of "His and Her Parent" Relationships*
◆ *Some Parents Compete for Couple's Love*
◆ *Cordial Relationships are Possible*

When two people marry, they each acquire a spouse, a set of parents-in-law, and brothers- and sisters-in-law. Likewise, the parents of the bride and groom acquire a child-in-law. What is not usually realized, however, is that these parents also acquire a relationship with the parents of that child-in-law.

In the Yiddish language, the two sets of parents call each other Machetunim, but there is no similar term in the English language to label this relationship. This may indicate that in our society little thought is given to this relationship. But term or no term, the relationship between his parents and hers does exist because the two sets of parents are tied together by a common interest — the welfare of their children and grandchildren. This relationship can take a variety of forms and involve a wide range of intensities: from warm, to lukewarm, to cold. The relationship includes feelings of: friendship, acceptance, competition, resentment, and dislike.

In my study, I uncovered three basic types of "his-and-her-parents" relationships, with variations in each type.

107

In the first type of relationship, his parents and hers may like each other and see each other frequently. Coming from similar cultural and religious backgrounds may help, as one woman expressed:

> Our cultural backgrounds are very similar. Our parents were both radicals. My parents-in-law see my parents even when we are not in town. They'll stop in for coffee, or they'll get together for dinner.

However, one set of parents may like the other set but does not socialize with them. Although they say they would like to be close with the other parents, they do not have the time or take the time to see each other. Their backgrounds and interests are different. As one parent put it:

> My son-in-law's family is delightful. We don't see them as often as I would like. I would like to get to know them better. You talk about nice people, and they are just the nicest. They give to their children, and they give to others. I often say, 'Let's go out to dinner,' but I don't follow through. I wouldn't say the relationship is close, even though they are really nice.

In the second type of relationship, one set of parents would like to see more of the other set, but the latter does not respond, as this woman said:

> We don't see each other much. To me it would make sense if they would call and keep in touch. We have so much in common: the children! About once a year, though, they have a family barbecue and invite me. I've made overtures to have a little continuity. It's just that they are not used to it. It's not meant personally. I don't feel slighted by this.

In a variation of this type, the two sets of parents may live too far apart to get to know each other or to get together socially. In another variation, visits may be infrequent and considered an obligation. In the following quote, both sets of parents live in Israel, but his parents come from Germany while hers are from Tunisia. Perhaps it is the cultural difference which explains the formal but distant relationship:

> When we meet, we are nice to each other, but we don't have much to say to the others except that we wish them well. They invite us to be with them twice a year, that's all. We're very correct, very friendly, but we live our lives and they live theirs. We don't try to get nearer to them. If we are invited, we come, we exchange greetings, and we might even exchange some presents — which is difficult because they are North Africans and very sensitive. When they give something that's worth a certain amount and you give them something that's worth a certain amount and you give them something that is worth less, it's a very sensitive issue.

In yet another variation of this type, the two sets of parents may get together only at the invitation of their children, as these men described:

> If there was a party, we invited both sets of parents. They weren't close, but they didn't dislike each other. There was no friction, and neither side hurt each other. At the beginning of my marriage, my mother-in-law made the first dinner, then my mother made dinner for them. But that was all. Now there's no friction and there's no friendship.

> The last time both sets of in-laws were in the same house was at the birth of my five-month-old son. Sometimes my parents visit my two sons and my mother-in-law drops in, maybe for 15 or 20 minutes in a face-to-face interaction. Or one of the in-laws calls on the phone and the other answers in my home. There's no set time formally when the two families get together — perhaps at a birthday party. Once a year, the in-laws will be in the same room for three hours munching birthday cake. Other than that, they are not together at any other time of the year. The common ground is the common grandchild.

In the third type of relationship, one or both sets of parents may not like the other. One man said: "My mother didn't like my wife and her whole family, and that's it." One woman's mother-in-law told her, "Just because you sleep with my son, what have I got to do with your parents?" Another man said:

> My parents will probably never accept my mother-in-law. The way my parents see my wife's mother is not as sophisticated, not cosmopolitan, not dressing well enough, not in the right social circles. My father judges people on their dress style and how they greet him and where they get money and where they went to the movie or out to dinner. I feel that at an unconscious level my mother also has a good deal of prejudice in her about who is acceptable and who isn't. Both my parents have a great deal of intolerance and probably project on in-laws what they don't like in themselves.

There are a number of possible reasons for dislike between sets of parents. Many people cited that the dislike stemmed from problems in planning the wedding, as did these people:

> I'll tell you what annoyed me. It comes from the question of finances, and it started with making thewedding.

> His mother's a widow. She caused me a lot of problems as far as the wedding goes. She's so flaky, and I can't say I appreciated what she did. We've never asked her out.

The first meeting between his and her parents evokes ambivalent feelings. On the one hand, there is joy when parents experience the happiness of their children; on the other, there is anxiety concerning the impending separation from that child. These anxieties can translate themselves as irritation focusing on money or on other issues regarding the wedding. Conflicting values and attitudes may come sharply into focus. One woman described this scene that was firmly etched in her memory:

> My parents and his parents were very suspicious of each other. I'll never forget the first time they were together. It was like a boxing-match interview. Both sets of parents were worried about how we were going to support ourselves. I think my mother was sort of

afraid that we would be dumped on them. She honestly believed that even though we were young, we should support ourselves. His parents felt that he should continue his education and that both sets of parents should continue to support us. Of course, none of them bothered to ask us.

Very often, a competitive spirit or a desire to impress is aroused in either set of parents. One woman reported how invigorated and energized she felt as she polished and painted her home to look and feel good in the eyes of the other set of parents. People want to make a good impression; this is healthy and desirable.

The birth of a grandchild may improve the relationship between the two sets of parents. One woman said, "When they had grandchildren in common, it gave them something to talk about." Conversely, it may also generate more competitive feelings between the sets of parents. One woman said:

> My father-in-law and my mother were friends for years, but when my son was born there was a whole issue of who he was going to be named for and who was going to hold the baby during the circumcision. My mother and my father-in-law actually had a fist fight! An actual physical fight! As if we had nothing to say about it.

Another woman reported, "When my parents buy my daughter a gift, my in-laws run out to do the same." One woman told her counterpart, "I got the dresser and crib, what will you get them?" Another woman said that the "other mother-in-law" would ask her at birthday time, "What are you going to give them?" and would always try to match her gifts. Frequently mentioned in this study was a concern about which set of parents was helping more: "They're very good to our daughter, except financially." "Our only disagreement is financial, the responsibility isn't shared."

These expressions of competition are similar to sibling rivalry. It is normal for each young child to want his parents all to himself, especially when a new brother or sister arrives. If the child does not feel comforted and reassured that his parents will love and care for him even when the parent's time must be shared, he will become jealous and competitive. These competitive feelings may be reawakened at the arrival of a grandchild. It is the reversal of the childhood situation. Now it is the grandparents who yearn for the love of their child. "The real tug of war," said one psychologist mother-in-law, "is who will be the most favored in love. I want my children to love me best."

Another reason for resentment between sets of parents may be feelings of possible loss of their child's affection. One woman suggested:

> Don't you think perhaps a mother and father of a daughter, although they like the potential son-in-law, who's going to take care of that daughter, may resent the family that's taking that daughter away from them? Maybe that's why they don't get along or don't want to get along.

An explanation for the conflict between the two sets of parents that cannot be ruled out is the theory of displacement. According to this concept, since it is not acceptable to resent a child's spouse, one may displace the resentment to that spouse's parents. One man described his feelings:

> It's a peculiar situation to begin with because you are compelled to associate with people whom you might not have chosen to associate with, and to embrace and take them in as an extension of your family. Being forced might induce resentment. I personally resent being compelled to undertake anything, and because I am compelled to embrace these people it becomes an effort to take them in by choice.

Many couples hope that after their marriage both sets of parents will be close to each other. One man said, "My wife thinks it's a nice adventure to expand your family." Another said, "It's nice to see that parents get along with the other set of parents." This, of course, does not always come about. One woman described her discomfort caused by tension between her parents-in-law and her parents:

I'm glad that they are in two different cities. When they are in a room together, I'm always watching to see how it is between them.

One man said, "I wish my parents would call hers when they come to town." Another woman said, "I would invite both sides of the family. It was never completely relaxed, but I persisted at it." Some couples accept the lack of closeness. One man said:

Well, my mother is not alone, she has friends and her own interests. She's that kind of person. I just wouldn't feel comfortable saying to my in-laws, 'Why don't you invite my mother over?'

Although the wish for a happy extended family may not be satisfied, the marriage may nevertheless remain quite solid. Whether the relationship between his and her parents will be good or bad, it generally will not make or break a marriage.

SUGGESTIONS

A relationship between you and your child's parents-in-law is not dependent upon how close they live, their economic status, or their religious convictions. Rather, it depends upon what other values and interests besides your children you both have in common.

Even though you begin as strangers, you need not continue to treat each other in that manner. Mutual respect, consideration, and communication will help to maintain a cordial relationship.

*Autumn is the mellower season, and what we lose
in flowers we more than gain in fruits.*

SAMUEL BUTLER
The Way of All Flesh

CHAPTER

XIII

In-Laws As Grandparents

- ♦ *Grandchildren Immortalize*
- ♦ *Grandparents Give Goodies*
- ♦ *Parents Don't Like Unasked For Advice*

A subtle change takes place in the young couple's perception when they become parents. The parents-in-law, who may have evoked images of grumpy, unsmiling, and critical people, evolve into "Grandpa" and "Grandma" with all the associated mental images of smiling, understanding, comforting and benevolent people. The negative in-law connotation, which may have partially caused the initial tensions may ease with the role change into grandparent status.

Some people view becoming a grandparent as one of their most important achievements in life, for it assures their immortality. One grandmother said, "A grandchild immortalizes you more than a child." Another said, "A grandchild means continuity. It's a guarantee for the future."

One young woman described how her parents-in-law's attitude toward her changed after she gave birth to their grandchild:

It's strange, once I became a mother and wasn't teaching anymore, my in-laws seemed proud of the fact that I had a Ph.D. I think they were worried, although they never said it to me, that I would turn out to be a career woman instead of a mother.

117

Upon the arrival of a grandchild, through birth or adoption, people begin to feel differently about themselves. One woman in this study said that she no longer thought of herself as a mother-in-law, but rather as a grandmother.

Many see the grandparent stage as another opportunity for self-growth. A college professor said, "I flubbed it with myself, I made even more mistakes with my children, but now I have a fresh start with my grandchild."

Others just get pleasure out of being a grandparent. One grandmother said her grandsons were her dividends in life. To baby-sit for them was her greatest pleasure. Many other grandparents reported similar feelings, that having grandchildren was one of the joys of life. The child-in-law and parent-in-law may also begin to feel and act differently toward each other. The son- and daughter-in-law may begin to feel more accepting of his parent-in-law as they shower his baby with attention and admiration. And the parent-in-law who formerly may have viewed his son-in-law as an outsider may now view him as the parent of his grandchild and therefore feel closer to him.

One son-in-law described these changes as follows:

I didn't know my in-laws too well before the baby. After the baby, it just seemed like all of a sudden I wasaccepted. There was a big difference. Before the baby I wasn't there much and didn't talk to them. Now I visit often, and we are a lot closer.

A daughter-in-law said:

It does change a relationship because there is a grandchild. I felt, 'This woman is the grandmother of my daughter.' There is some cementing there, for sure, just as my mother-in-law must have felt, 'This woman is now the mother of my grandchild.' I think my mother-in-law was able to be much more giving and establish a closer relationship with me once there was a grandchild. Before that, she was much more reserved.

Yet another woman pointed out, "When I saw how giving they were to my child I felt differently toward my in-laws."

Parents often need physical and financial help, as well as advice, in raising their children. Grandparents who are sensitive and responsive to these needs are greatly appreciated. At times, a parent may discover that his parents-in-law are even more helpful and generous than his own parents.

One daughter-in-law said:

> I could not ask my parents for help when I was younger. My parents had seven children, they just didn't have anything left over for my husband and me. But I always felt I could ask my in-laws for anything and they would be there. If I was sick with the babies, they would be there as soon as I called.

Another said:

> I wish I could take my babies to my mother, but she is a working woman. Besides, she has remarried and her husband doesn't care for my kids. But my mother-in-law will take care of them and looks forward to taking them.

One woman asked her mother-in-law to counsel her teenaged daughter:

> Tell your granddaughter what is on your mind. If you don't like the guy she is going with, feel free to share what you feel. It might be better coming from you than from me.

Young parents may feel disappointed when the grandparents do not live up to their expectations as the "ideal" grandparent. One young mother said:

> I think my mother-in-law is missing a good time with my kids. She could have established a relationship, and she's never done so. I know if she just came and hung around for a few hours she could talk more with them. They are terrific kids. I'm resentful in view of the fact that she has nothing else important to do with her time.

Young parents may also be irritated when the grandparents do what the parents think they shouldn't. One woman said: "I wish she wouldn't feed them cheeseburgers and candy."

The parents are also angered when they feel criticized by the grandparents (and criticism of the grandchildren is often construed as criticism of the parents). They may also be irritated by grandparents' suggestions on how to raise the grandchildren, interpreting these suggestions as criticism. One young mother explained:

> You're newly on your own, trying to assert your independence and make your way in the world. Suggestions from in-laws are not as easily taken in the beginning as they are later.

Another said, "A lot of people think when they are older they have the right to tell you what to do." A man said, "My in-laws were critical of the way we reared the children. They thought we gave them excessive religious training."

Young parents need understanding and encouragement, not continual criticism. A parent who feels constantly disapproved of and criticized may be reluctant to spend time with the grandparents, thus widening the physical and emotional gap between them. One daughter-in-law said:

> My in-laws would say, 'Oh, the poor child is so pale, so pathetic...he's starving.' I took it all seriously and internalized a lot of their comments and became very resentful of them.

A working mother complained:

> My mother-in-law feels that her grandson has to come first, that if I took upon myself the responsibility of having a child, then my life has to be for my child. I resent it when she tells me, 'You stay home because the baby comes first.'

The criticism need not be verbalized. These mothers had similar reactions to implied criticism:

My mother-in-law always wanted to know why the baby wasn't wearing the dress she bought.

I purposely would not give my mother-in-law the satisfaction of seeing my daughter wear the clothes she gave.

The relationship between the parents and the grandparents can affect how the grandparents relate to the grandchildren. One grandparent described it this way: "If you don't get along with your son-in-law, then you don't get to see your grandchildren. They become estranged to you." Another said, "When my son saw I did not accept his wife, they purposely moved out of state." Even if the parents don't move away, the grandparent may hesitate to get close to the grandchild if he doesn't get along with the parents. One grandmother said:

I felt inhibited from playing with my granddaughter when I was in my daughter-in-law's presence. I felt a wall within myself that kept me from enjoying her.

The grandparent may dislike or even become hostile toward the grandchild, as these women recalled:

I know my grandmother didn't like me and my mother. She always told me to wash my face, comb my hair. I always felt unacceptable to her.

As a child, I remember my grandmother was always critical. She kept telling me my teeth were crooked, or I should have the mole taken off my face, or I should stop jumping on the bed.

This grandmother's hostility toward her grandson may have been due to her distrust of herdaughter-in-law:

I'm sure of my daughter's child — I saw it grow in her belly. But how can I be sure of my son's child?

Another woman expressed a similar doubt about whether her son was really the father of her grandson, since her daughter-in-law was pregnant before they were married. Suspicions about the grandchild's paternity may cross many grandparents' minds, and though they are rarely verbalized, they can adversely affect the in-law relationship and the relationship with the grandchild.

In contrast, a grandparent may dislike his child-in-law, yet be loving and supportive to his grandchild.

The relationship between the parents and the grandparents can also affect how the grandchild relates to his grandparents, as these men described:

> My grandmother had negative feelings about my mother. I don't know if it affected my grandmother's attitude toward me, but I know definitely it affected the way I felt about my grandmother.

> Even though the mother doesn't realize what she is doing, she teaches her children to resent the other side of the family. It's not done maliciously or purposely, but you kind of grow up with that slight resentment of the other side.

Sometimes the grandparent's behavior has nothing to do with his feelings about his grandchild, or his child-in-law. People have other responsibilities and interests, and this realization may be a disappointment to the young couple who expect the grandparent to be exclusively devoted to his grandchild.

Grandparents can fail to achieve the ideal "wise, understanding and giving" grandparent status for any number of reasons. They may still have young children of their own, as this 45-year-old grandmother said:

> I'm still involved in parenting of my own children. My son is 11, and my daughter is 9 1/2. I have responsibilities at home and can foresee being pulled in two directions when my daughter-in-law asks me to babysit. If your own younger child comes home and asks you to take her somewhere and here you are stuck with a baby, you are pulled. It's a conflict that you did not purposely create.

They may be glad to have finished parenting their own children and be reluctant to give up their freedom to do what they want when they want, as this grandmother said:

> I'm sick of responsibilities for animals or kids. I'm not ready to be a doting grandmother. I don't want to take care of my grandson.

They may be preoccupied with their own concerns, such as health and career, as well as marital and financial problems, as was this woman:

> I have grown-up children. I have in-law children. My health is waning. I'm constantly torn by the role expectation. I'm not the traditional grandmother. I wasn't the traditional mother. I don't have guilt feelings, but I'm not fulfilling the roles my children want of me.

They may be struggling for financial security or for a new identity after divorce or death of their spouse. A 42-year-old grandmother starting a new career whispered: "Shhh! I don't want people at work to knowI'm a grandmother," because being a grandmother would label her as an older woman.

Another group of grandparents who may show even less interest in the grandparent role are the very old. One daughter-in-law said:

> My mother-in-law was a little old lady, quite feeble and sick. Both sets of parents were old and let us alone.

Though grandparents may not fulfill the role of an "ideal" grandparent, parents and grandparents should try to understand each other's needs and desires in order to share the pleasure that comes from responding to the needs of loved ones.

A FURTHER NOTE

Grandparents are sometimes refused the right to visit grandchildren whose parents are divorced. To rectify this, a bill has been introduced in Congress "establishing the right of grandparents and grandchildren to have access to one another." However, legislation only focuses on the symptoms, not the disease. The symptoms are the refusal of visitation rights, but the disease is the antagonism between grandparents and their children-in-law.

No one would disagree that grandchildren and grandparents are important to one another, but until now the underlying in-law tensions have not been examined. In light of this new legislative thrust, it is appropriate to examine these in-law tensions. Then perhaps grandchildren will no longer be used as pawns in the conflict between grandparents and their children-in-law.

SUGGESTIONS FOR GRANDPARENTS

Try not to criticize the way your child and child-in-law clothe, feed, or raise your grandchild. Though they might need your physical and financial help, they do not need unsolicited suggestions, no matter how wise or helpful you feel they are. It is their child and their turn to raise him in whatever manner they feel is appropriate. Also announce your visits, don't drop in unexpectedly. Empathize with the young parents — remember how it was when you were a young parent.

SUGGESTIONS FOR PARENTS

The arrival of a new baby is an exciting and demanding time in your lives. The baby constantly needs your physical and emotional attention. In addition to this emotional pressure, having a child also brings financial pressure and you may have to ask your parents and parents-in-law for financial and/or physical help. If they provide help, be sure to express your appreciation. If you feel that they are being too helpful and perhaps even intrusive, respectfully set limits. Above all, don't make unreasonable demands on their time — they have raised their own children, and it is now time for them to enjoy themselves and their grandchildren.

It is seldom indeed that one parts on good terms,
because if one were on good terms, one would not part.

MARCEL PROUST
The Fugitive

CHAPTER
XIV

Ex-In-Laws

♦ *What Do You Call Them?*
♦ *Are They Still Family? No Rules For Relating*
♦ *Post-Divorce Relationships Vary*

With the steadily growing number of divorces, more and more people are becoming ex-in-laws, and how to relate to them is even less clearly defined in our culture than how to relate to in-laws. Sharing experiences, joyful as well as sorrowful, bonds people emotionally. Thus, over time, whether an in-law is liked or disliked, he becomes a meaningful part of the family. A divorce may legally and physically break up a marriage, but it does not immediately break up these emotional bonds.

In a short, unhappy marriage in which the in-law relationships may not have had time to develop, the rupture of the in-law relationships may not be very traumatic. One woman in this study who was married only a year said:

> I had too much of a problem with my husband. I didn't have time
> for my in-laws. My marriage was such a short-lived entity,
> nothing developed. My ex-in-laws mean nothing in my life.

However, in some short marriages where the in-law interactions and involvements have been close, the divorce may result in hostile reactions among family members. Another woman who was

127

married only a year but who felt that she had had a close relationship with her sister-in-law said:

> I made the error of thinking my sister-in-law was a friend of mine. When I called to talk to her about our getting divorced, she never returned my phone call. I felt that she wasn't my friend, even though she had pretended to be.

In long marriages where the interactions have led to a deep involvement, the rupture may be very traumatic and painful, regardless of whether the relationship was friendly or antagonistic. One woman said:

> Since the divorce, I'm a non-entity. My in-laws and I had a good relationship when I was married. We were good friends. I was closer to them than to my own parents. It took me a long time to stop crying when they shut me out of their lives.

Most in-law relationships are built little by little, just as a sweater is knitted stitch by stitch. At a divorce, this relationship begins to unravel until all one has left is worn-out emotions, like a skein of used yearn. What was once a warm, comforting sweater is now a collection of string. The relationship that was once so palpable and important leaves only residues of hurt feelings and memories. For example, children of adivorced couple may be eternal reminders of an ex-in-law by their physical resemblance to that person.

Ex-in-laws are faced with the same types of problems they had during their marriage. For example, what do you call the ex-parents-in-law? How do you introduce an ex-son-in-law or an ex-father-in-law? "I don't want to be introduced as an ex-anything," said one woman. "Ex means you're wiped out. I'd rather be introduced as a friend.' Another woman calls them, "former in-laws."

Another type of problem arises at holidays, birthdays, graduations, weddings, or other family get-togethers. Is an ex-in-law still considered part of the family, and if so, for how long? Should you invite the ex-spouse of a close family member to a family affair? What if that family member objects? "If you invite my ex-wife to the bar-mitzvah," one man said, "I'm not coming."

A third type of problem is visits, either casual or formal. If you have been meeting your mother-in-law or father-in-law for lunch or golf regularly before your divorce, must you now stop these visits? What if your ex-spouse disapproves? One woman, for example, said that her ex-husband phoned her to ask her not to meet his mother for lunch anymore.

Another problem is gift-giving. Should you continue to send birthday cards and gifts to an ex-in-law? What about grandchildren? What about giving financial aid when it is needed or requested? One woman who received no child support from her ex-husband turned to her ex-father-in-law, a millionaire, to help her pay an emergency medical bill for her son, his grandson. The ex-father-in-law refused saying, "It's not my problem." Though she finally got help from her ex-brother-in-law, she still doesn't understand why her ex-father-in-law wouldn't help: "He can never use up all his money. Why couldn't he help his grandchild? I wasn't asking for myself."

In contrast, another woman offered her ex-daughter-in-law a $1,000 loan when she overheard her saying that her home needed tuckpointing.

People relate to their ex-in-laws in varied ways:

Some remain friendly. This woman described how her family continued to like and be supportive of her ex-sister-in-law:

My sister-in-law was a good-hearted person who was kind to my mother, and after the divorce she lived upstairs at my mother's for five or six years. We felt close to her even after her remarriage.

A father told his divorced son: "All the wedding pictures are staying right up there on the walls. This is my house, and she's still my daughter-in-law.

One woman initiated contact with her ex-daughter-in-law.

I wrote my daughter-in-law a letter to say, 'Now that I'm not your mother-in-law anymore, I hope we can be friends.' When I saw her after that, she said she wanted to call me by my first name and we should be friends.'

Some sever their relationships. Many people feel uncomfortable in the presence of a person who is no longer a member of the family. They may feel slighted, hurt, or angered by the rupture of the relationship and robbed by the changes that take place during and after a divorce. Since it is easier to blame the divorce on the ex-in-law, they may break off all contact with him. Parents may feel disloyal to their own child if they continue to show any interest in the ex-in-law. Even if they feel that their own child contributed greatly to the divorce, they may nonetheless be loyal to him to the extent of refusing to see or speak to the ex-in-law.

The ex-child-in-law may still desire to remain friendly but accept the fact that things are different now. One woman said:

> I tell myself I'm not the daughter-in-law anymore, but I still feel part of them, not separate from them, not yet. I have the desire to see them but not the need.

Some become more understanding after a divorce. A woman who had felt competitive and uncomfortable with her mother-in-law realized after her divorce how young and immature she had been:

> I was too young and not sure of myself. It was my inability to accept their constructive criticism or praise. I never heard the praise. It was said, but I was unable to accept it because I didn't have positive self-respect.

It is understandable that many people want to avoid contact with an ex-in-law because of the many feelings that are stirred up. Nevertheless, it seems a waste that the bonds of friendship that are so often created between in-laws must be harshly and abruptly severed when a divorce takes place.

SUGGESTIONS FOR EX-PARENTS-IN-LAW

Just because your child did not get along with his spouse, that is no reason to sever connections with your former child-in-law. You may feel disloyal to your child if you keep up the friendship, especially if your child objects, but the decision as to whether or not to maintain the friendship is yours. Do not let your divorced child decide for you.

Grandchildren are an important reason to maintain a friendship with your ex-child-in-law, whether they live with your child and more especially if they live with your ex-child-in-law. It is important to both you and the children to remain connected. Don't underestimate the emotional benefits to yourself and your grandchildren in maintaining this relationship. We all need the loving warmth of responsive family members.

SUGGESTIONS FOR EX-CHILDREN-IN-LAW

Just because you and you spouse did not get along, that is no reason to sever connections with your spouse's parents if you like them, and especially if there are grandchildren. Don't let the anger you may feel for your ex-spouse prevent you from maintaining a relationship with them. The situation may be awkward, especially if your ex-spouse is opposed to your maintaining a relationship with his family, but it may be worth the effort.

Widows, widowers, and divorcees may find it helpful to seek counseling before remarriage. Doubled-up families may benefit from discussing their apprehensions, resentments, and new arrangements.

How do you deal with an in-law?
Buy a house by a river and ask them to drop in.

A friend's sarcastic advice

CHAPTER

Strategies
For Coping

- ♦ *Sort Out Your Feelings*
- ♦ *Talk Things Over*
- ♦ *Are You Part of the Problem?*

The traditional advice that parents-in-law give to other parents-in-law regarding problems with their children-in-law is to mind your own business, don't interfere, bite your tongue, let them live their own lives, don't say anything. Similarly, the traditional advice that children-in-law give to other children-in-law regarding problems with their parents-in-law is to tolerate them, suffer through, don't even try to change them. Such advice encourages the distancing of the generations. Wise though it may be at times, it doesn't always get to the heart of the problem of understanding what is actually going on.

Usually what is going on is that a parent-in-law or child-in-law feels misunderstood, hurt, criticized, or intruded upon by the other person. To improve relations, you need to take a good objective look at yourself and at your in-laws. There is always more than one party involved in a misunderstanding.

Though there are no magical formulas for doing this, the following suggestions may help you deal with your in-law problems:

Step 1: Sort out your feelings about your in-laws. Do you feel misunderstood, hurt, criticized, disappointed, rejected by them?

What have they done to make you feel bad? Have they insulted, ignored or offended you? Were your suggestions rebuffed or your invitations ignored? Have they slighted you by not answering your questions or respecting your privacy? Try to pinpoint exactly what they did or said to offend you. Remember that a slight to one's self-esteem can hurt more than a physical injury.

Step 2: Talk about your feelings. Ideally, the person to talk to about the slight or injury you experienced would be your spouse. An understanding spouse can be of great help in getting along with your in-laws. Be aware your spouse may be sensitive and take criticism of his parents or siblings as criticism of himself.

The next best person to talk to is the in-law in question. Pick an appropriate time and place when neither of you is rushed. Be tactful. Even though you may offend the other party, be very explicit about your problem. For example, "I'd like to talk to you about something that's been bothering me. Why don't you write thank-you notes when I give you a present?"

This is easier said than done, however. It took one woman 14 years before she could talk to her father-in-law about a problem that only he could solve — his not waiting for her to sit down to dinner before he starts to eat.

If you can't talk to the other person, try to determine what keeps you from doing so. Analyzing the matter in this way may help you overcome this barrier. For example, you may be reluctant to discuss your slight because you may think it's no use, they won't understand. Or you may think it is not respectful to confront your elders with your hurt and possibly offend them. Or you may not feel sure enough of yourself to do so. Or you may be so overwhelmed by the hurt that you cannot even talk about it.

If it doesn't help you to talk to the in-law in person, it would be better to talk to another trusted person such as a close relative or friend. Often, people are afraid to talk about in-law problems with a relative or friend for fear that it will get back to the in-law involved. In such a case, a therapist is a valuable alternative.

Regardless of whom you choose to discuss your problems with, sharing your thoughts with a caring person who will listen closely and nonjudgmentally is as necessary as oxygen is for breathing. To be understood makes you feel worthwhile and may help heal the hurt.

I repeat, do not underestimate the power of good manners. "Simple politeness and graciousness are equal to wind and water in changing matters" (unknown author). Good will created by good feelings diminishes in-law tensions. "A soft answer turneth away wrath" (Proverbs). Words and the tone of voice in which they are said may make a difference and ameliorate tensions.

Step 3: Look deeper into yourself and consider how you might be contributing to the problem. It is easier to blame others than to think that you may have been at fault.

Have you offended your in-laws in any way? Have you been brusque and impatient? Have you had unreasonable expectations about being treated in certain ways? For example, did you expect gifts from your in-laws at special occasions? Did you expect to be phoned or visited frequently? Have you had preconceived ideas that in-laws would be intrusive and inconsiderate? Our society is full of stereotypes about in-laws as troublemakers.

How have your family's history and attitudes regarding in-laws affected your attitudes and expectations? Think about your experiences as a child. Did in-laws get along in your family?

Grandmothers and grandfathers are idealized in stories and literature, but they are also mothers and fathers, aunts and uncles, sisters and brothers. The patterns of interaction with these people make powerful impressions on the child and may influence present behavior and feelings. Remember what you didn't like about them. Remember what you wanted to change in those situations. A therapist may be helpful in this step.

Step 4: Realize that there may be cases in which the in-law with whom you are concerned is emotionally ill or extremely unreasonable and no amount of talking will help. In such a case, avoidance may be the best approach. The point is not to blame yourself but to give yourself credit for having tried to make the relationship work.

Most of the suggestions I have offered relate to empathy and respect. Empathy means to be able to *understand* another's needs and feelings; respect means to be *considerate* of those needs and feelings. It is important to have empathy and respect for your in-laws, but it is equally important to have empathy and respect for yourself. If you empathize with and respect your in-laws' feelings without understanding or respecting your own, you may find yourself becoming angry and dissatisfied. Conversely, if you care only for your own needs and feelings without considering and understanding those of your in-laws, they may be angry and dissatisfied.

Most in-law problems will resolve themselves when you and your in-laws have acquired mutual understanding and respect. I hope that the suggestions I have given in this book will help you and your in-laws achieve this goal.

*If you examine the problem closely enough,
you see how much of the problem you really are.*

One of Murphy's Laws

XVI

When to Seek
Professional Help

◆ *"Psychopathology" Means "Hidden Difficulties"*
◆ *Recognize Symptoms That Indicate You Need Help*
◆ *Seeking Help Does Not Mean You Are Mentally Ill*

During the interviews conducted for this book, I heard many vignettes about positive relationships — in-laws who came to be caring and supportive. I also heard about destructive relationships — in-laws who were insensitive, sadistic, and emotionally disturbed.

Those who are experiencing the first type of relationship need little advice, except to fully enjoy your friendly in-laws. But those who are experiencing hurt and pain in dealing with your in-laws may need to seek help from a psychiatrist, psychologist, clinical social worker, psychotherapist, or clergyman trained to understand and explain what is happening. You will thereby begin to feel better about yourself and your in-law relationships.

Some difficult in-law problems defy common-sense solutions because they mask hidden difficulties — psychopathology — brought into the marriage by one or both of the marriage partners or their parents. Only with the help of psychotherapy could one young woman, for example, who felt enraged about her mother-in-law, come to see that she was equally enraged with her own mother who had died and "left her" when she was a little girl. Another woman

141

realized during her treatment that her disappointment in her mother-in-law was similar to the feelings she had felt earlier in life toward her mother who was so critical. In both cases the rage and disappointment with their mothers-in-law began in their early child-parent relationships.

Good will is not enough to improve a destructive in-law relationship. If you recognize any of the following reactions, it might be helpful for you to see a psychotherapist for help: (1) You find yourself continually thinking and talking about your in-law problems. (2) You feel so overwhelmed by your problems that you simply don't know what to do. (3) You are afraid to discuss your problems with your spouse, relatives, or friends for a variety of reasons. These reactions do not mean you are mentally ill, but it may indicate that you need a professional to understand and explain these strong, stressful emotions.

Dealing with a blatantly sadistic or devious in-law can make you feel that you are falling apart, and/or that something is wrong with you. You may need the services of a psychotherapist to deal with such distressing feelings as anger, frustration, or helplessness. An example of one such sadistic in-law's behavior happened one New Year's Eve when a mother-in-law phoned her son and daughter-in-law to tell them, "Dad is in the intensive care unit at the hospital, please come home, and we'll all go to the hospital together." The young couple, fearful and worried, drove as fast as they could for three hours on the icy highway to see the father as soon as possible. When they walked in the door they saw Dad sitting on the couch with Mother — both of them grinning. Mother said, "We knew this was the only way we could get you to come home on New Year's Eve."

Another insensitive mother would only ask her son over for breakfast or send but one ticket to a ballgame so that her son could attend without his wife. In these situations, the son refused the invitations and sent back the ticket. But frequent instances were reported where a young man would see his parents first before seeing the wife after work or would eat with his parents instead of having supper with his wife. In the first instance, the mother could use some help, and in the second instance, the young man is still merged with his parents and could use the services of a professional to help sort out his seemingly inappropriate loyalties.

Still another situation that indicates the need for psychological help is when illicit sex occurs between the in-laws: for example, fathers-in-law having sexual relations with their daughters-in-law, or brothers-in-law with sisters-in-law and nieces, or fathers-in-law with grandchildren. Mothers-in-law who are seductive with their sons-in-law are another source of embarrassment and humiliation in the in-law relationship.

Those of you who are feeling unhappy with yourselves or your in-laws — whether the source of this emotional discomfort lies within you or is caused by your spouse or his parents — don't be ashamed to turn to a qualified psychotherapist for help. If unattended to, these bad feelings may accumulate and grow, causing continual hurts that fester, and may possibly result in physiologic symptoms such as colitis, ulcers, migraine, asthma and other ailments.

People who are trained in this area of psychotherapy include psychoanalysts, psychiatrists, clinical and psychiatric social workers, psychologists, and some members of the clergy. For further information on how to contact these people, contact your local hospital, medical association, or mental health association.

If you've tried your best to improve your in-law relationship and nothing helps — not gracious manners, talking to a friend or therapist — stop trying, or obsessing. Give the in-laws space. Even the best army retreats sometime. You may be dealing with incorrigible in-laws who will not or cannot change. Take heart, however, some do change: A 103-year-old woman recognized that she was an awful daughter-in-law, but 40 years later she admitted she had become a better mother-in-law.

Get involved with people and causes that make you feel good.

Neither good nor peace can come from strife.

Sefrei on Deuteronomy 21:10-21

CHAPTER

XVII

The Last Will
And Testament

- *Who Gets What and Why*
- *Leaving People Out of the Will*
- *Giving to Grandchildren*

Sooner or later parents must consider how to dispose of their worldly goods. Usually parents intend to leave most of their property, money, or mementos to their children as gifts. But parents who have been offended and disappointed by their adult children and sons- and daughters-in-law may feel conflicted about what to leave to whom. Some parents described their quandary: "Shall I take my son and daughter-in-law out of my will?" asked a 75-year-old woman. For the past ten years she had asked her son for pictures of her grandchildren and great-grandchildren, to no avail, yet he repeatedly asked for loans to expand his business. A 66-year-old woman adds codicils to her will whenever she gets angry at her son-in-law and daughter. A widowed mother was worried, "How do I safeguard money that I want to leave to my daughter from my son-in-law who will smoke dope and drink it away?"

How do parents solve relationship difficulties and gift giving at this late date? To avoid future problems, one mother asked her adult children and in-laws to tell her which household items — furniture, pictures and/or knick-nacks — they wanted. One woman who realized her son-in-law will never change his drinking or drug habits consulted a lawyer to safeguard her money for her grandchild.

Before another woman wrote her son out of her will, she wrote her son and daughter-in-law "a letter of forgiveness" to ask forgiveness for any unintentional hurt she caused.

One man whose daughter-in-law does not allow him to visit his grandchild said, "You desire to give to your children, but there is a pain that never should have been, and there is nothing you can do." He decided not to exclude them from his will. The anguish of chronic in-law problems may follow some parents to the grave — they feel too immobilized to make a will.

Howard N. Gilbert, a lawyer who practices in the state of Illinois, stated that most of his clients don't leave their children-in-law any money. Instead they put the money in trust, so their child has an income, and then they make sure it goes to the grandchild. If the adult child dies before the child-in-law, an appointed trustee makes sure the money goes to the grandchild, not the in-law.

Some sons- and daughters-in-law are not interested in an inheritance. "I didn't want anything from them before or after they died," said one woman. Others appreciate what their spouses receive. One son-in-law said, "My wife deserves it for all that she did for her parents." To distribute the family silver left by his mother, an oldest son divided the silver items equally by weight, numbers and lots. All his siblings and their spouses agreed to accept whichever numbered lot they drew.

Other sons- and daughters-in-law greedily anticipate the inheritance before the parent-in-law dies. A woman, married to the "only" son in the family frequently phones to push her sister-in-law to remind her mother, "Make sure your mother's 'will' includes a double portion for the only son."

Whether you are disposing of your worldly goods or inheriting some, consult a competent lawyer. Inheritance laws may differ in every state of the union. Do not make your decisions in a fit of anger.

MORE SUGGESTIONS

Because a will is a legal matter, consult a lawyer whom you trust and is competent in the area of estate planning. Decide what you want to do about your money and property and your grandmother's silver and china. Make a list of all that you want to give away. Take the list to a lawyer who will put your money and property in a will or trust arrangement that will accomplish what you want. Your will must clearly define what you want to give to whom.

Consider giving some of your money away as gifts while you are alive. Consider donating some of your money to charitable organizations.

Anytime anything happens be prepared to update your will — not just because you are angry — but because a new baby is born or people die. Even if there is an immediate blood relative to whom you don't want to leave anything, consult a lawyer. You may have to leave him something so he will have no possible claim against your estate.

For those who wish to improve their in-law relationships before the last will and testament, rereading chapters XII, XVI, and XVII may help.

Empathy, the recognition of the self in the other, is an indispensable tool of observation, without which vast areas of human life, including man's social behavior in the social field, remain unintelligible.

HEINZ KOHUT, Pilgrimage,
The Journal of Pastoral Psychotherapy,
Vol. 5, No. 1, 1977

XVIII

Self Psychology
and the Theory of In-Law Relationships

- ◆ *At Last a Theory to Explain In-Law Tensions*
- ◆ *How Theory was Uncovered*
- ◆ *Respect and Empathy are the Keys to Diminish Tensions*

A. INTRODUCTION — THE VALUE OF SELF PSYCHOLOGY IN APPROACHING THIS SUBJECT

Social scientists and mental health professionals who have been involved in individual therapy and in studies of family relationships have written very little regarding "in-law" relationships. This lack in the professional literature was undoubtedly due in part to the absence of a psychological framework by which to explain or to understand these relationships.

The theory of self psychology, the psychoanalytic study of self during growth and change, as developed by Heinz Kohut, M.D., has broadened our perspective on many subjects, including that of "in-law" relationships.

The "self" is a composite of the experiences, memories, impressions, and feelings that a person has had of himself from childhood on. This composite also includes a person's view of himself in the present and the future. To have a sense of well-being, the self needs "selfobjects." These are people, or objects (including pets) that function, and are experienced, as part of the self and

153

contribute to the self's development. They serve to keep the self feeling whole and well. They provide a constancy during change so that the self does not fall apart.

Parents are the child's first selfobjects. They soothe him, protect him, and help him grow emotionally. Without their reliable presence, admiration, and encouragement, the child may not develop adequately. Similarly, the child is a selfobject for the parents, making them feel good about themselves.

The relationship between the parent and the child is one of the closest of all human relationships. When the child marries, this relationship changes. The parent may feel as though he is losing a selfobject, while the child is acquiring a new selfobject, a spouse. While these changes take place, all parties concerned may feel off balance and out of sorts.

Thus, the transition of becoming an in-law causes changes and imbalances in the self and its selfobject relationships. This makes the self more vulnerable to slights and insults and may result in feelings of hurt, anger, rage, or depression.

In some cases, becoming an in-law is not experienced as a disturbance, just as in some exceptional cases giving birth causes no pain to some mothers. But in the majority of cases, becoming an in-law does cause tensions related to the disruption in the selfobject relationship.

People need a supportive network, especially during times of change. Though the form of this need may change over a period of time, it will never be outgrown.

B. THE RESEARCH STUDY

Because of the dearth of research material, I undertook an exploratory, descriptive study of in-laws. To get specific in-depth feelings from the respondents, I conducted unstructured interviews, beginning with this question, "What is it like to be an in-law?"

I interviewed men and women of varying ethnicity's, socio-economic levels and occupations. These people included Afro-Americans, Arabs, Armenians, Bahamians (both black and white), Canadians, Chinese, Cubans, Ethiopians, Greeks, Irish, Israelis,

Italians, Jews, Mexicans, Nigerians, Pakistanis, Poles, Russians, and Swedes. Interviews which were scheduled for 45 to 90 minutes were usually conducted on an individual basis, with an occasional group session. The following findings draw on responses to more than 250 taped interviews.

C. THE IN-LAW THEORY

I posit that becoming an in-law causes a series of normal, transient, age-appropriate disruptions of the self in both parents and children. These disruptions cause tensions and discomfort.

There are similarities in becoming a child-in-law and in becoming a parent-in-law — both encounter disruptions. But one thing is different: children never had parents-in-law before, while parents have already had the experience of being children-in-law. This earlier experience, whether pleasant or unpleasant, may influence the parents' behavior toward their children-in-law.

1. The Child's Perspective

A person's marriage causes a normal disruption in the relationship he has had with his parents. Initially, a child psychologically experiences his parents as a part of himself. What he wants or needs is supplied by his parents, as if upon command. Little by little, the child learns to do for himself that which the parent has done for him, such as admiring, calming, soothing. As the child matures, he absorbs and modifies the ideals, values, and ambitions of his parents. Since a person never outgrows his need for self objects, his need for his parents is deeply imbedded in his self.

As the child's self grows more cohesive, his connection to his parental self objects gradually decreases, and his connection to other self objects — siblings, peers, teachers — gradually increases. One of these new self objects is a spouse. The child's ties to his parents thus become attenuated but not severed as he forms his new relationship with his spouse.

There are many disruptions that may occur as a couple's relationship develops:

Each newlywed may realize that the mate has ties to his/her family. He may feel unsure about her relationship with him and need reassurance that her feelings for her family do not take priority over her love for him. He may thus feel jealousy and hostility but may hate to admit to them since they spoil one's self-image.

The bride and groom's jealousy and hostility may eventually subside. What occurs is similar to parents reassuring a small child after a new brother or sister is born — as the parent reassures the child that he is stillloved, the child's jealousy and hostility diminish. The bride and groom are not small children, yet each still needs reassurance from his mate and acceptance from his parents-in-law. Then, jealousy and hostility may decrease. However, if the bride and groom do not feel affirming acceptance from each other and the parents-in-law, tensions and competitive feelings may remain.

There are other ties that may cause feelings of divided loyalty between spouse and family. Is he disloyal when he visits his wife's parents? Whose family shall they visit at holiday time, his or hers? Whose family shall the husband and wife name the baby after? Whose family should they live near? How much should they spend on gifts for each family? Whose values will prevail regarding religion or schools? Archaic feelings for the earliest self objects — the mother and father — sometimes remain, and the parents may intrusively tug at these feelings with phone calls and invitations and expectations.

The adult child experiences a redefinition of his self-image. He is no longer single but married. He must accept the reality of a mate who may or may not fulfill a life-long fantasy. He must come to grips with the reality of being responsible for the welfare of another.

The necessity of dealing with a whole new family at the critical moment when the bride and groom must focus on each other in order to fulfill the dream of beginning a new life is not simple. The relationship with this new family may be burdensome, or the newlywed may find that he receives more and better emotional support than he has ever had before. In either case, whether the relationship is burdensome or pleasing, it is a disruption to adapt to.

When the newlywed's ideals and values match those of his parents-in-law, all is well. But if the ideals and values are different and there is no respect for the differences, there may be tensions. Disrespect and insensitivity increase the possibility of slights and hurts. Even if the newlywed and parents-in-law have different value systems, there can still be harmony if they are respectful of the differences.

2. The Parents' Perspective

Parents also undergo disruptions. When their child marries, their relationship to their child is sharply altered. They are no longer as needed as they had been before.

It is obvious that parents are important to children, but it is not as obvious that adult children are important to parents. Adult children not only provide sources of esteem for parents, but also expose parents to new ideas. Furthermore, the child gives to the parent a sense of fulfillment and satisfaction.

Parents have spent years providing for the physical and emotional needs of the child. As the child matures, he contributes to the parents' self-esteem and growth. As child analyst Anna Orenstein stated, "The conception and birth of a child reopens the adult's self development and constitutes a potential for further development, consolidation and expansion of the adult self." Being a parent is thus an opportunity for continuing enrichment and refinement of the adult self.

When a child gets married, parents experience joy and pleasure. However, they also temporarily experience a disruption, a sense of loss of part of the self. The loss is two-fold — physical and emotional. It is physical because although the child may have moved away earlier, he is now even less accessible to the parent. It is emotional, because the child will not be as available to make the parents feel needed, proud, and vital. Neither will the parent receive as much attention from the child as he did before the child's marriage. The expression, "You're not losing a daughter, you're gaining a son," reassures the parent that he has not really lost the relationship with his child.

It takes time for the child to feel confident enough in his marriage for the relationship between parents and child to resume at the previous level without seriously disrupting the relationship with his spouse. It also takes time for the parent to view the child-in-law as a member of the family.

Many parents overestimate their child's abilities. Sigmund Freud used the phrase, "His majesty the baby," to describe this parental overestimation. Parents may even extend their fantasy about their child's worth to his mate. They may dream of greatness not only for the child but also for the mate. If a child chooses someone who seems close to this fantasy, the parents are pleased. But disruption occurs if the child-in-law does not reflect the parents' values, yet must be taken into the family. The parents feel that by loving this person, their child has slighted them by abandoning their values. These slights to their self-esteem hurt more than physical pain. If, however, a child-in-law's behavior and attitudes are similar to those of the parents-in-law, it becomes less disruptive and easier for parents to welcome him into the family.

Upon becoming a parent-in-law, a person experiences an internal disruption of his self concept and to the ways he views his child. It may take time for the parent to come to the realization that he is no longer the parent of a small child but the parent of a mature adult.

He is therefore no longer young. A change also takes place in the ways he views his spouse — he may now see his spouse as an aging person. For some, this conscious awareness of time passing may be very disturbing, and may even interfere with sex for a time.

It should be emphasized that the inevitable move of the child into marriage is natural and healthy. Nevertheless, it temporarily upsets the parent's self-balance.

D. CONCLUSIONS

This study bore out my view that in-laws are important people in our lives and that an understanding of in-law relationships would be helpful. The results of my research may be described on two levels — a universal level applicable to many cultures, and a personal level.

On the universal level, I uncovered commonalties that apply to most in-law situations. The commonalties include a pattern of events or transition points — the first meeting, the wedding preparations, vacations and holiday visits, the birth or adoption of grandchildren, etc. — at which times the participants are most vulnerable to tension and stress.

I reaffirmed my belief that a successful in-law relationship requires a deliberate effort to understand each other and to communicate with each other. Only then can the relationship become warm and close.

I learned that an ingredient for successful in-law relationships is the ability to respect the young couple's need for privacy. Parents who make demands for equal time, equal visits, equal gifts, etc., make it difficult for a young couple.

I found that competition and resentment between his and her parents exist at the beginning of the marriage. Such tensions may escalate before the wedding but subside later as people regain their equilibrium.

I felt assured that the married couple remain connected to their parents and siblings after marriage. Whether they see each other frequently or even like each other, they know about each other's activities and whereabouts through the family grapevine. Even if the couple dislike the in-laws, they often benefit from the family ties through financial aid, gifts, and other benefits, material and emotional, which serve to make the recipients feel secure, whole, and good about themselves.

And on the personal level, I learned to respect my children and children-in-law, distance myself from them, and admire their uniqueness as they build their lives together.

I have not composed this work to teach people what they do not already know, but to remind them . . . of what is well known to them indeed. For most of what I say is nothing more than what most people do know.

MOSHE HAYYIM LUZZATTO
18th Century author of *The Highway of the Upright*

XIX
POSTSCRIPT

Since my last book I became a mother-in-law three more times and a grandmother 15 more times. I have gone a long way toward making fewer mother-in-law mistakes. Currently I am researching the subject of friendship. Had I studied the topic sooner I would have said that to become a good in-law requires the same skills it takes to become a good friend. It is a joint, deliberate, respectful, sensitive process whereby you learn about one another. It takes time and effort to listen and accept the other as he or she is. Just as close friends do, good in-laws make you feel good. Satisfying in-law relationships do not just happen. If you are lucky and wise you may help it happen.

QUESTIONNAIRE

The following questions are provided to help you evaluate and understand your own in-law relationships. If you wish, you may send — anonymously — a completed copy of the questionnaire to Leah S. Averick, c/o Lifetime Books, Inc., 2131 Hollywood Boulevard, Hollywood, Florida 33020-6750 for use in my continuing study of in-law relationships. Your comments and suggestions are also welcome.

LEAH S. AVERICK

Section 1
MOTHER-IN-LAW — FATHER-IN-LAW

If you are, or have been, a mother-in-law or father-in-law, please complete the following section, Questions 1 through 46. Please answer even if your in-laws are no longer living.

1. What would you like your son/daughter-in-law to call you?

2. Why did you choose to have your son/daughter-in-law call you this?

3. Do you feel you get along well with your son/daughter-in-law?

4. How many sons-in-law do you have?

5. If more than one, do you like one son-in-law more than the other? Why?

6. How many daughters-in-law do you have?

7. If more than one, do you like one daughter-in-law better? Why?

8. Do you get along better with your sons-in-law or daughters-in-law? Why?

9. What do you like most about your son/daughter-in-law?

10. What do you like least about your don/daughter-in-law?

11. Do you get along well with your son/daughter-in-law's parents?

12. Do you want to see more or less of your son/daughter-in-law's parents?

13. How long have you been a mother/father-in-law to each of your children's spouses?

14. Have your attitudes toward your son/daughter-in-law changed over the years? How?

15. Do you like your son/daughter-in-law better than your own child?

16. Have you ever helped your married children financially?

17. How do you feel about giving your married children financial help?

18. Have you ever helped your married children in other ways? How?

19. Does your son/daughter-in-law come to you for advice?

20. Do you feel comfortable in your son/daughter-in-law's home?

21. How often do you visit your married children in their homes?

22. How often do your married children visit you in your home?

23. Do your married children see you often without their spouses?

24. Do you feel comfortable dropping in on your married children without prior notice?

25. Do your married children visit you on holidays? Which ones?

26. Do you feel your visits with your married children and their spouses are good, bad, boring, etc.?

27. Do you hold a job? ___ Full-time ___Part-time
                        ___ Neither

28. Do you have any outside interests (i.e., volunteer work, hobbies, clubs, etc.)?

29. How many children do you have? Boys _____ Girls _____

30. How many of your children are married?
    Boys _____ Girls _____

31. Do you feel close to your daughters or your sons? Why?

32. Do you feel closest to a particular child?

33. If you feel closer to one particular child, do you think this affects your relationship with his/her spouse? If so, how?

34. Did you approve of your child's selection of a mate?

35. If not, what were your objections?

36. Do you feel your son/daughter-in-law is good for your child?

37. Do you have grandchildren? How many?

38. Do you feel your son/daughter-in-law is a good parent?

39. If not, why not?

40. Do you prefer to visit your child without seeing his/her spouse?

41. Do you argue frequently with your son/daughter-in-law?

42. What are the issues you argue about most often?

43. Does your own child get involved in arguments between you and your son/daughter-in-law?

44. Do you keep arguing about the same issues, or are there new ones?

45. What kind of person did you expect your son/daughter to marry?

46. Were you disappointed in your child's selection of a spouse? If so, why?

Section 2
SON-IN-LAW — DAUGHTER-IN-LAW

If you are, or have ever been a son-in-law or daughter-in-law, please complete the following section, Questions 47 through 96. Please answer even if your in-laws are no longer living.

47. What do you call your in-laws?

48. How did you come to this decision?

49. Do you like your in-laws?

50. Do you like one of your in-laws more than the other? Why?

51. Are your in-laws divorced or widowed? Do you feel this affects your relationship with them? If so, how?

52. What do you like least about your in-laws?

53. What do you like most about them?

54. Do your parents get along with your in-laws?

55. How do you feel about the relationship between your parents and your in-laws?

56. Have your in-laws ever helped you financially? If so, how do you feel about this?

57. Have your in-laws helped you in other ways? How?

58. Can you come to your in-laws for advice and assistance?

59. Do you feel comfortable around your in-laws, or are you constantly on your best behavior?

60. Do your in-laws visit your home frequently?

61. Do your in-laws visit you without an invitation? How do you feel about this?

62. How far away from your in-laws do you live? If very far, how often do they visit you and for how long? How often do you visit them?

63. How far away from your parents do you live? If very far, how often do they visit you and for how long? How often do you visit them?

64. Do you have children? If so, ages _____

65. Has having children of your own affected your relationship with your in-laws? If so, how?

66. Do you communicate with your own parents frequently?

67. How often do you talk to your in-laws?

68. Do you work outside the home? _____ Full-time _____ Part-time
_____ Neither

69. Do you have other outside interests (i.e., volunteer work, clubs, etc.)?

70. Did you work before marriage? If so, what type of job?

71. Does your spouse defend you when you argue with his/her parents?

72. Does your spouse try to become involved in your arguments with his/her parents or siblings?

73. When you have an argument with your spouse, does it affect your relationship with your in-laws?

74. Do you defend your parents in arguments they have with your spouse?

75. Do you feel your spouse supports your feelings about his/her parents?

76. How does your spouse feel about your parents?

77. How does your spouse feel about his/her parents?

78. Do you feel your marriage is excellent, good, average or poor? Why?

79. Does your relationship with your spouse affect your relationship with his/her parents or siblings?

80. Do your in-laws ever sleep overnight at your home. If so, where do they sleep?

81. When having both sets of parents for dinner, who is served first, second and third?

82. Do you feel your in-laws interfere in your day-to-day routine? How?

83. Do you feel your in-laws interfere in your marriage. How?

84. Did your in-laws approve of your marriage? If so, why? If not, why not?

85. Has your relationship with your in-laws changed over the years? How?

86. Do you feel your in-laws could be a serious threat to your marriage? If so, why?

87. How long have you been married?

88. Is this your first marriage? If not, do you get along with your first set of in-laws? How do you feel your relationship with your first set of in-laws influenced your current situation?

89. What are your recollections of your parents' attitudes toward their in-laws? Do you feel this affected your attitude toward your in-laws?

90. Do you feel accepted by your in-laws? If not, why not?

91. Do you feel rejected by your in-laws? If so, have you tried to remedy this situation? In what ways?

92. Did you live together before marriage. If so, do you feel this affected your relationship with your in-laws? How?

93. How did you expect or hope your in-laws would treat you?

94. Did your in-laws meet your expectations?

95. Were you disappointed by your in-laws? If so, why?

96. Have your in-laws been a major problem in your marriage? Please explain.

Section 3
BROTHER-IN-LAW — SISTER-IN-LAW

Please answer questions 97 through 108 if you have a brother-in-law or sister-in-law. Please answer even if your in-laws are no longer living.

97. Does your spouse have any brothers or sisters? If so, how many?

98. What did you expect or hope your relationship to be with your new brother/sister-in-law?

99. Did you relationship turn out to be the way you thought? If not, why not?

100. Do you get along with your spouse's brother? If not, why not?

101. Do you get along with your spouse's sister? If not, why not?

102. Does your brother/sister-in-law affect your relationship with your spouse's parents?

103. Do you have any serious problems with your bother/sister-in-law? Explain.

104. Are there any other in-laws who cause serious problems for you? How?

105. Does your brother/sister-in-law get involved in arguments you have with your spouse?

106. Does your brother/sister-in-law get involved in arguments you have with your in-laws?

107. Do you feel your in-laws compare you to your brother/sister-in-law?

108. Do you feel your in-laws compare you to your brother/sister-in-law's spouse? If so, how do you feel about this?

Section 4
STATISTICAL INFORMATION

Please complete the following information to the best of your ability. All information and answers will be kept strictly confidential.

109. Sex: Male _____   Female _____

110. Age: Under 20: _____   20-25: _____
              26-30: _____   31-40: _____
              41-50: _____   51-60: _____
              Over 60: _____

111. Ethnic background: Please explain your family ethnic background to the best of your ability, including race and religion:
     Mother's side: _____
     Father's side: _____

112. What religion to you consider yourself to be:

     _____

113. What religion were you raised in? _____

114. Do you practice your religion? _____

115. Are you American born? _____

116. Are your parents American born? _____

117. Are your in-laws American born? (Please specify which in-laws are not.) _____

     _____
     _____
     _____

118. Please check all that apply. Are you a:
     Mother-in-law _____   Father-in-law _____
     Daughter-in-law _____   Son-in-law _____
     Sister-in-law _____   Brother-in-law _____

119. Educational background (please check all schools which have
     been completed):
     Grade school _____   Junior college _____
     High school _____   College _____
     Vocational school _____
     Professional school _____
     Graduate school _____

120. Is this your first, second, third marriage? _____

121. Do you have children? _____ Ages: _____

122. Are you separate, divorced, or widowed? _____

123. What is your yearly income (regardless of source):
     Under $10,000: _____
     $10,000-$19,999: _____ $20,000-$29,999: _____
     $30,000-$39,999: _____ $40,000-$49,000: _____
     $50,000 or over: _____

REFERENCES

Benedek, Therese (1970), Parenthood During The Life Cycle. In E.J. Anthony, ed. with T. Benedek, PARENTHOOD, ITS PSYCHOLOGY AND PSYCHOPATHOLOGY, Boston: Little, Brown & Company.

Freud, Sigmund (1914), On Narcissism: An Introduction. In STANDARD EDITION, vol. 14, London: Hogarth Press.

Goldberg, Arnold (1973), The Psychotherapy of Narcissistic Injury. In ARCHIVES OF GENERAL PSYCHIATRY, Vol. 28.

Kohut, Heinz (1977), THE RESTORATION OF THE SELF, New York: International Universities Press.

Mauss, Marcel (1967), THE GIFT, New York: W.W. Norton & Co.

Orenstein, Anna and Orenstein, Paul (1985), Parenting In The Adult Self. In E.J. Anthony, ed. with G. Pollock, PARENTING INFLUENCES: IN HEALTH AND DISEASE, Boston: Little, Brown & Company.

Spielrein, S. (1913), Der Shvigermuter. In IMAGO, edited by S. Freud, Vienna: Hugo Heller & Cie.

Wolf, Ernest (1983), Selfobject Relation Disorders. Edited by M.R. Zales, CHARACTER PATHOLOGY, New York: Brunner/Mazel, Inc.227